DESIGNING & BUILDING
Rockhill and Associates

Tuns Press
Faculty of Architecture and Planning
Dalhousie University
P.O. Box 1000
Halifax, Nova Scotia
Canada B3J 2X4
tunspress.dal.ca

Designing & Building: Rockhill and Associates

Editor: Brian Carter
Design Consultants: Bhandari & Plater Inc.
Production: Donald Westin
Printing: Friesens

© 2005 by Tuns Press
All Rights Reserved. Published December 2005
Printed in Canada

Library and Archives Canada Cataloguing in Publication

Rockhill and Associates / Brian Carter (ed.).
Includes bibliographical references.
ISBN 0-929112-53-9

1. Rockhill and Associates.
2. Architecture-Kansas-20th century.
3. Architecture-Kansas-21st century. I. Carter, Brian, 1942-

NA737.R62A4 2005   720'.92'2   C2005-902827-0

The publication of this book was supported by a grant from the
Graham Foundation for Advanced Studies in the Fine Arts

DESIGNING & BUILDING
Rockhill and Associates

TUNS PRESS

Contents

Foreword

GRANT WANZEL

Since its inception, the *Documents in Canadian Architecture* series has aimed to "produce documents that offer an insight into the process of design by documenting the '*facts*' and the products of the process: the sketches, drawings, and the end products… in a way that is unobscured by unnecessary rhetoric or biased presentation" and is "free of the publicizing and advertising tendency that so often haunts such publications." The work then would stand on its own, fully exposed to critical reflection and serious study.

A laudable objective, a difficult path and an elusive goal to be sure. Occasionally though, when the winds have been just right and everything else was in good order, we've come close; the magic achieved by virtue of a committed staff in close combat with a talented editor, and a selfless practitioner. The early publications were remarkably spare. The projects were well documented and relatively few in number. The black and white photographs and drawings were stark and the accompanying text was factual, almost cryptic. But it worked well and was well received.

With this publication we've allowed ourselves the luxury of extensive colour. A first for us. We've also opened the door to a colleague who is not Canadian and who lives and works in a country that is not Canada. Another first. But Dan Rockhill is a soul-mate. His architecture is place-specific to his adopted Kansas and has much in common with the works we've published previously. Colour, light, texture, and material quality are also major considerations in all of his buildings. This is much in evidence in his lush photography and helped to convince us of the need for colour in the book. Dan Rockhill is a talented designer/builder whose work also presented us with a new challenge: how best to represent a body of work in which the processes of its creation as well as the artefacts themselves are of importance? Our redress has been to a prolific use of illustrative photographs, drawings and explanatory text.

Most of us at Dalhousie University have not seen his buildings first hand, but we have met the man. Dan Rockhill was one of several invited lecturers to speak at our 2003 Professional Practice Module. He spoke passionately and convincingly of his work; of the importance to it of the place, its landscape and cultural history; of making, of teaching and learning, and of learning by making. He illustrated his topic "Design/Build in Practice" through reference to his extensive body of work as a designer, builder and educator. His work struck us as edgy, risky, and highly ambitious, seeking simultaneously to operate on many levels and in several realms. Our aim in this publication therefore is to reveal the processes and levels that are at play in his architecture. And to show how his work as builder, educator and architect are all parts of a single body.

George Bernard Shaw once wrote of the crime of indifference as being far worse than the crime of hate. Dan Rockhill's architecture is deeply engaged and engaging. It's anything but indifferent. It can be witty, amusing and impish. It's always inventive. Sometimes it seems a little over-the-top, when by Dan's own admission it risks becoming frivolous, even self-indulgent. But it could never be accused of indifference. Rockhill, his students and colleagues take great pleasure in the making, in its spontaneity and in the sharing of their pleasure with those who can in turn take pleasure in the result. Never satisfied, Dan Rockhill seems always to be pushing the limits. On the other hand, it appears his architecture is becoming more composed and more at ease with itself. Rockhill's work is all about processes – building, conserving, making, learning, teaching, and taking and giving pleasure. In this regard, it is work that gives as good as it takes.

Almost Hidden from View

BRIAN CARTER

"The dividing line between high and low culture is utterly fictitious. Genuine culture is neither high nor low; it involves ideas you're happy to keep returning to for the rest of your life" [1]

Ideas encountered beyond traditionally accepted boundaries and across cultures frequently influence architecture. The impact of such ideas can be traced through the writings of Deleuze and Foucault to the development of de-constructivism while the effects of digital media are readily detectable in the current projects of the 'blob meisters'. The work of other architects has been inspired by influences as diverse as the geological detail of land-forms, film, the potential of material, and the supposed vitality of the commercial strip. In presenting his own approach to design the architect Dan Rockhill readily identifies the significance of America's mid-western agricultural landscape as an inspiration for his work.

Agriculture in America was, Benjamin Franklin noted, "the great business of the continent" [2] and later, Thomas Jefferson made more ambitious claims when he suggested that the United States would 'remain virtuous… as long as agriculture is our principal object." [3] Rockhill lives and works in Kansas where land in the eastern part of the state was plotted by surveyors and settled by farmers early in the nineteenth century. With the passing of the Homestead Act in 1862, others subsequently moved west across the state to take up more territory for cultivation.

In the same year that the Homestead Act was passed Christian Schussele completed a painting entitled 'Men of Progress'. Portraying "the most distinguished inventors of this country, whose improvements… have changed the aspect of modern society, and caused the present age to be designated as an age of progress" [4] this painting acknowledged the significance of agriculture in America. Cyrus Hall McCormick, Henry Burden and Isaiah Jennings, all inventors of new equipment to improve farming, were included in that group and, as if to further underline the importance of farming, Schussele also painted a model of a proposed new mechanical reaper into the foreground of his painting. The design, production and distribution of these new farm machines were pursued aggressively and the ploughs, reapers and mechanical rakes patented in the mid nineteenth century were quickly followed by tractors, balers and combine harvesters that enabled farmers to develop extensive systems of cultivation that transformed the land. These inventions also placed the new and sophisticated machines alongside simple buildings built to house the American farm.

These transformations initiated by the mechanization of agriculture prompted the invention of other machines. Silos, grain elevators, windmills, fuel tanks and storage bins created new mechanized infrastructures that were made of metal, fabricated in factories and shipped across the country. This sophisticated equipment was plugged into sheds to create collages of machines and buildings that caught Rockhill's interest.

Seeking to record this agricultural vernacular Rockhill photographed the places in ways that recall the work of Bernd and Hilla Becher. The interest of these two artists in everyday industrial structures – water towers, blast furnaces, coal bunkers, ore mines, steel mills and the like – has produced an impressive and systematic collection of carefully composed records. However, their readily identifiable grids of black and white photographs shot from set vantage points reveal more than the mere constructional detail or architectural form of these indigenous buildings. For example the Bechers' images of the wooden mineheads, or 'coal tipples', built by jobless miners in the wooded foothills of Appalachia, not only record these flimsy temporary structures and provide opportunities to compare the ingenuity of their design and construction but also provoke other responses. So the tipples "have an aura about them like craft, or art. We want to 'read' into them. As anthropological artifacts or as art, for example, they express a lot about a local economy based on individual or family enterprise and a self-reliant way of life in general… tell us about the spirit and something of the physical character of this region" [5]

Rockhill's collection of photographs of agricultural buildings in Kansas captures the ongoing vitality of life on the farm. Assembled over many years, his is a collection that records small modest vernacular buildings, many of which are still in use in the vast rural landscape of the American plains. Images of houses, outbuildings, sheds, small shops and barns are placed alongside others showing grain silos, oil tanks, crop sprayers and farm machinery in ways that highlight old and new, reveal both landscape and buildings, show equipment and the occasional animal, trace marks of human activity and note the impact of weather.

The designs of Dan Rockhill also consist of small buildings and machines. Most are new but some are historic structures that he and his team have helped to carefully restore. All are local to where he works. They use familiar materials and are in places where the weather is extreme. Some are in towns but others have been built in wide flat landscapes of the plains. Yet each has been carefully sited with an eye for the climate and constructed with a directness that recalls the insight and ingenuity of the farmer and conspicuously references the American farm.

As well as exploring the contrast between simple buildings and intricate machinery Rockhill invents machines. Sometimes they have been designed to respond to special circumstances. At the Shimomura-Davidson Studio, the heavy rainfall from sudden summer storms typical in this part of Kansas is collected and discharged by a series of galvanized hoppers and sculpted chutes. Integrated with frames that support overhead garage doors and opening mechanisms, this is an assembly that readily recalls the pragmatism and ad-hoc forms seen in nearby farm buildings.

In other projects this architect sites the machine in the garden. Balconies, staircases and canopies become elaborate metal machinery that stands alongside archetypal houses. The machine also re-appears inside the building as conspicuous industrial components and moving parts are used to make up the bathrooms and kitchens. Sometimes the machine almost takes command. In the Epard/Porsch House a series of steel roofs above stone clad buildings are elaborated to create distinct towers and moving shelters for outdoor viewing platforms while screened porches for domestic rooms are housed on metal platforms and stairs made to fold and move. Suddenly living rooms are transformed into spaces that recall grain hoppers and barns or shaped as if to reference the fantasies portrayed in drawings by Lebbeus Woods.

Commissioned by clients to design a series of small buildings in one specific area of the country Rockhill has also been able to develop a particular way of working. By building these projects as well as designing them he has not only been able to stretch budgets and achieve high standards of workmanship but expand the design process to encourage experimentation, take in searches for new materials and consider the ingenious recycling of others. It is an approach that elevates the act of construction beyond predictable need and defines an agenda where design, fabrication and construction are equally valued in the furthering of a program of research that explores the potential of materials, economy, costs and time.

Other projects have been developed as a part of an educational initiative. As well as working as an architect in practice Rockhill, in his role as a teacher at University of Kansas, created Studio 804 in 1996. It is a program that provides opportunities for teams of students to design and build a small inexpensive house for a needy family each academic year. The program has seen the construction of seven new houses on different infill sites in and around the town of Lawrence. In sharp contrast to the standardized house plans and conventional wood-framed construction systems used by 'Habitat for Humanity' these houses explore a wide range of materials and techniques. Each house is different from the other. It is an approach that connects two different ideas in architectural education. One highlights the learning that accrues from not only designing but

making – the development of new understandings of material qualities, cost, the disciplines of constructional systems and building codes as well as the impact of weather, weight, fabrication and time on design and architecture. The other projects a view of design as a participatory exercise and as a service that is aimed at directly improving the quality of life for both the individual and the public at large regardless of income.

A group of recent projects – the Newton House and a Wedding Pavilion set in rural Douglas County, together with an addition to an existing restored historic building in Lawrence completed in the last three years – represent a significant development in Rockhill's work. Unlike the self-conscious juxtapositions of buildings and machines that typify earlier projects the impact of the machine in these recent schemes is evident systemically. For example, while the design of wood and canvas structures developed for a pavilion built for a day-long wedding ceremony explores the use of 'as found' materials it also reworks those materials through the precision of machining and the order of systematic assemblies. Consequently these are not examples of wild individualism or the wood-butcher's art but constructions that recall the communal effort and energy of a barn-raising. They also reflect an urgent quest for lightness that suggests the machine. It is a lightness that appropriately underlines temporality through the design and use of materials so as to capture the dignity, spontaneity and celebration of a very special occasion at a significant place on a family farm.

The two other projects – the rural house and the urban kitchen – are both permanent buildings. The house is free-standing and sited in the expansive open landscape of Kansas while the kitchen is built into a relatively constricted urban site and connected to an existing historical stone building. Both are constructed largely of metal and glass. Both demonstrate a thoughtful combination of new building and servicing machine, but the use of conspicuously manufactured, machine-made components in both projects is countered by over-arching concerns of construction and performance. The systematic nature of construction seems, in these two buildings, to organize those components into a larger whole – a move that contrasts with the seemingly free-wheeling bricolage and dramatic gestures of the earlier work. In the design of the urban kitchen this larger whole is made even larger because of the house that not only already exists on the site but which forms the basis for the entire project. The transformation of this house with the making of a new garden by the addition of an elegant free-standing glassy pavilion integrates building and machine, old and new, site and setting. The use of materials and the details of their assembly are clear and underline the benefits, skill and commitment of architects who both design and build.

The work of Dan Rockhill, his associate David Sain and their many colleagues and assistants is modest in scale. Embedded in the vast agricultural landscapes of Kansas and backstreets of Lawrence, it is almost hidden from view. Yet it is work that is significant. It is a testimony to the value of design, the difficulty and arduousness of building and to the importance of the deep-seated potentials of architecture to change and improve the lives of people.

1. Hugh Kenner, *The Elsewhere Community* (Don Mills, ON: House of Anansi Press, 1997). Kenner's book was based on his 1997 Massey Lecture at the University of Toronto.

2. "The Internal State of America," in *The Works of Benjamin Franklin*, vol. 2, ed. Jared Sparks (Boston: H. Gray & Co., 1836), 462.

3. December 20, 1787. From *The Life and Selected Writings of Thomas Jefferson*, ed. Adrienne Koch and William Peden (New York: Modern Library, 1944), 441.

4. *Americans: Paintings and Photographs from the National Portrait Gallery, Washington, DC* (London: National Portrait Gallery, 2002), 88.

5. Bernd and Hilla Becher, *Pennsylvania Coal Mine Tipples* (New York: DIA Center for the Arts, 1991). Foreword by Charles B. Wright.

An Architecture of Resistance

JUHANI PALLASMAA

In the current culture of affluence and abundance, materialism and obsessive consumption, quasi-rationality and nostalgia, architecture has become threatened. The art of architecture is curiously marginalized by two opposite tendencies: instrumentalization and aestheticization. On one hand, buildings are seen as mere instruments of simplistic functional performance and shrewd profit making, and on the other, as objects of visual seduction speculating either on the conservatism of taste, or images of superficial novelty. The escape to numbing nostalgia and the false authority of styles is alarming. This architectural fundamentalism is supported by respected universities, corporations and civic institutions as well as private clients and neighborhood associations. The nostalgia for the past reveals a split in our collective sense of reality and a weakening of self-identity. In the consumer culture, identity is increasingly purchased through consumption, and social prestige is acquired through the borrowed aura of falsified history.

The negative effects of these collective pre-occupations on architecture are further reinforced by a weakening sense of materiality and tectonic reality as well as the disappearance of craft. Increasingly, the touch of the human hand is lost. Standardization, propagated by modernity, has become a mixed blessing, and as a result of the insensitive application of mass produced and aesthetically unsatisfactory components, architecture has frequently degenerated into simplistic assemblies devoid of artistic passion, skillful construction and technical innovation.

Literature, music and film have divided into two distinct categories: serious art and entertainment. It is a division that is also evident in architecture and nowadays much of the search for experientially and existentially meaningful architecture takes place in small studios rather than the production lines of corporate offices.

Confidence and hopefulness about the future are prerequisites for the emergence of authentic architecture. That architecture also calls for idealization; significant buildings always project an idealized image of both the individual client and the prevailing cultural condition. Meaningful architecture is conceived for an idealized client projected and internalized by the architect himself. This does not, however, imply self-centeredness or a lack of reality on the part of the designer. Rather it projects a confidence in the continued refinement of culture and human qualities. The task of architecture is to work towards a more cultured humanity and an emancipated society.

In America Frank Lloyd Wright's visionary Usonian houses, which represented a genuinely American architecture, and the products that grew out of the Case Study House program of the *Arts & Architecture* magazine continue to radiate optimism about the future, a joy of life and the courage of new visions. These delightful houses are reminders of the utopia of modern architecture that a pioneer generation of modernity envisioned. And although the vitality and passion of those projects are still vital today, those houses, and the ideas that prompted them, have never become part of a widely accepted lifestyle.

The pessimistic condition of architecture has given rise to pockets of resistance around the world. This movement has a confidence in the architecture's humane cultural mission, and it defends the autonomy and authenticity of architecture against the erosive forces of global culture. Characteristically, compatriots of this resistance seem to create a worldwide set of shared concerns, values and aspirations.

Dan Rockhill, an architect who is living and working in America, has established a determined liberation front of architecture that is in opposition to the conditions that marginalize the feasibility of meaningful and dignified dwelling and construction.

Rockhill builds modest and reasonable houses for ordinary clients at surprising low cost, and preserves humble, yet significant buildings of vernacular history. These restoration and renovation projects include the Constitution Hall in Lecompton, one of the

oldest existing wood frame structures in Kansas, Hollenberg Pony Express Station, the only remaining station from the history of the Pony Express, Fort Hays Blockhouse, built in the 1860s to provide protection for railroad workers and supplies to forts in western Kansas, and the Beaumont Water Tower, the last wood and steel tower of its kind in the United States. Rockhill's architectural mission is to restore these fragments of the past and put them in a dialogue with authentic images of our own time.

Instead of following universal architectural fashions, he has looked to the vernacular traditions of the American prairie for inspiration. Instead of today's intellectual abstractions, his buildings are informed by farming constructions, such as barns, grain silos and agricultural machinery, or the early mechanical imagery of railways – steam locomotives, train stations and water towers. Instead of the separation of the construction site and design studio that is common to architectural offices today, Rockhill constructs his designs himself with his own construction crew.

Instead of nostalgic domesticity, he is interested in archetypal methods of place-making and relating the dweller with the landscape and forces of nature by means of architecture. "Here, the house," he claims, "is a simple form inspired by the common industrial and agricultural buildings that dot the landscape. They are elementary objects that rest between the earth and the sky, contrasting with both. In this open land the vertical and horizontal are profound." [1]

Anonymous vernacular architecture develops gradually through trial and error to seek a perfect response to climate, function, material and structure. This gives rise to images of unselfconscious but irresistible beauty. As Joseph Brodsky assures us: "Beauty can't be targeted, it is always a by-product of other, often very ordinary pursuits." [2]

Rockhill's buildings are set in a vivid dialogue with their settings. They echo the vast grassy expanses of the mid-western landscape. Sometimes his structures derive from historical precedents, as the central structure of the Terrace House in Baldwin, Kansas, which was inspired by the log structures of the Pawnee Indians. Rockhill also often utilizes generic American house types, such as the 'shotgun' and 'dogtrot' plans, workshop and loft structures. His buildings evoke the open horizon and high skies of the Kansas landscape. They are modest, reflect a sense of tradition, and recall prairie fires, wagon trails, buffalo, early industrial installations and railways.

Like traditional vernacular structures, Dan Rockhill's buildings seek an ecological rationale. His architecture aims to balance thermal extremes through architectural means, utilize the cooling effect of winds and breezes, and recycle materials and building components in a manner that combines environmental concerns with the artistic idea of assemblage and the ready-made. Salvaged steel trusses, grates, sash, cabinets, steel ladders and veneer stone – all are scrutinized and often used.

Dan Rockhill's architecture returns to that particular pragmatic way of thinking, praised by Alexis de Tocqueville 150 years ago in his study of the American character in *Democracy in America* and articulated later by that country's pragmatist thinkers. His design/build operation re-connects the conceptual, intellectual and abstract dimensions of design with the skill of the hand and the inherent logic of construction. His buildings are not ideas hatched in the intellectual ambience of an architectural office; in his working method, the concrete reality, materials, crafts and processes of making inform architectural thought and vice versa. The architect does not only conceive forms, he also devises efficient ways of building. In addition to bypassing the frustrating technical and aesthetic limitations and increased costs brought about by conservative and unambitious building contractors, Rockhill's design/build approach facilitates genuine innovation. It is an approach that also re-connects with the early history of architecture, where architecture arose from facts of construction rather than autonomous visual ideas.

In his revolutionary and heroic task of creating the dome of the Duomo in Florence, watchmaker Filippo Brunelleschi had to conceive an entirely unprecedented engineering structure to realize his formal architectural vision. He also had to devise machines for moving huge blocks of stone great distances, and elevating them to the dizzying heights of the dome.

Characteristically, Rockhill's project descriptions are laconic matter-of-fact reports of the architectural and technical solutions with little reference to philosophical speculations or artistic intentions. In fact, his project descriptions often include meticulous reports of execution processes. His architectural language is based on the expression of structure, and rugged materiality combined with refined details, transparency and translucency. In his architecture, austerity, outspokenness and clear-headedness turn into aesthetics, and reason turns into poetry. On the other hand, Joseph Brodsky sees a primary or a priori value in the aesthetic judgement, as he writes: "Man is an aesthetic being before becoming an ethical being." [3] This interaction of aesthetic values and ethical concerns is evident in Rockhill's architecture. Prosaic realities, such as collecting rain water and directing it from the roof to the ground, are poeticized; a practical requirement is turned into a sensory delight. Functional and technical causalities reinforce the experience of the real and create a sense of rootedness.

In his buildings, a simple volume acts as the ground, against which canopies, balconies, staircases, louvers and windows read as visual accents and foreground objects. Appropriately to their relation with vernacular traditions, his houses are formally simple. The Epard Porsch House, however, presents a rich, articulated, fragmented and slightly deconstructivist appearance. The metaphoric telescope shape of the library suggests motion, whereas the observatory tower is equipped with a roof cover that actually moves. Mechanical parts, such as stairways rotating by means of pulleys and counter-weights,

translucent partitions moving on wheels and rails that are clearly visible, and the kitchens and bathrooms that he has designed recall the Maison de Verre in Paris, designed in the late 1920s by Pierre Chareau, Bernard Bijvoet and Dalbet, the locksmith. Rockhill's technological aesthetics refer to passionate and lyrical examples of early modernity, rather than today's cool, perfected and often alienating High-Tech.

Rockhill's houses are devoid of traditional gestures of domesticity and instead frequently suggest an industrial imagery, as the western façade of the Shimomura/Davidson-Hues Studio, and the barrel-vaulted shape of the Newton House. In fact, Rockhill's houses question and challenge the notion of home. Echoing those revolutionary houses of modernity, his houses suggest that home can be devoid of all inherited architectural symbolizations and be a device, a *machine á habiter*, through which the dweller is rooted in the world. In the words of Gaston Bachelard, the French philosopher of architectural imagery, the house "is an instrument, with which to confront the Cosmos." [4] This metaphysical task is engaged with the act of dwelling and distribution of a place, the center of one's world, rather than with any given formal images. The experiences of being protected, looking out into the landscape, entering and exiting, sitting by the dining table or next to the fireplace, taking a bath, or resting in one's bed, are all verb-like encounters which constitute the essence of dwelling and home. In fact, 'at homeness' acquires its special emotive power through these primordial encounters rather than from conventionalized and emotionally empty symbols. Instead of recycling bourgeois conventions, Rockhill's architecture seeks to revitalize our primary experiences of nature and dwelling.

In an absolute contrast to his usual industrial imagery, the chapel for a wedding that was made of cottonwood trunks and built on a grassy field in Kansas evokes the primordial structures of mankind, and native Indian rituals. The reception hall with its suspended

lamella arch and membrane cover projects a contemporary and technological counterpoint to the primordial note of the chapel. The two structures define a specific place in the same ritualistic way as the ancient Roman military camp or the mobile settlements of nomadic cultures.

Rockhill's executed projects are in rural settings, mostly domestic and utilitarian in character. His project for the headquarters of the CORE Advertising Agency in St. Louis successfully expands the realm of his approach to an assured and elegant urban office building. The project combines structural and constructional rationality and sensuality, clarity and a sense of youthful excitement appropriate for a company operating in a creative field. In accordance with the architect's conceptual metaphors for the CORE project, 'beehive' and 'sponge', the building is a space for spontaneous interaction without hierarchy, receptionist, fixed work stations or separate rooms for individual employees. The space is organized by means of a series of vertical towers that contain lights and numerous power and communications connections.

Rockhill's relentless confidence in his mission seems to have earned him more critics as well as supporters in his immediate surroundings. The spray-painted warning by an angered neighbor or bypasser on the concrete wall of one of his buildings, "Paint this or I will," [5] is an example of this conflict of tastes and values. "It gets to the point, where I'm almost afraid to use my own name to order a pizza," [6] he confesses regardless of his tough and determined character. The opposition evoked by his simultaneously rugged and refined, reasonable and poetic buildings, brings to mind Glenn Murcutt, the Australian architect who has gradually gained global recognition in spite of a series of court cases related to his work prompted by conservative regulations and local attitudes.

In his role as professor at the University of Kansas in Lawrence, Dan Rockhill passes his beliefs, passions, skills and experiences on to younger generations. The Studio 804 is a workshop that he has organized within the architectural program of the university. It has produced several remarkable small houses designed and built by architecture students for low income and disadvantaged citizens through local non-profit organizations. These houses are products of student thinking and work, but they are also part of Dan Rockhill's personal architectural mission, as they directly reflect his beliefs, aspirations and strategies. "We believe in making environments that are accessible to anyone, not only in a physical sense, but also monetary. We believe that creative young minds can make a difference in the affordable housing community and that we can dispel the notion that architects only provide services to the advantaged." [7]

In our time, when architecture at large has lost its social mission, celebrated avant-garde architecture has often become mere narcissism, and academia is hypnotized by intellectual and formal games, this ethical credo has a special weight and significance. Regardless of the pessimistic view of today's cultural condition, architecture continues to have the framing of human life and provision of a horizon of significance and meaning as an essential task.

1. Dan Rockhill, project description for the Newton House.

2. Joseph Brodsky, *Watermark* (London: Penguin Press, 1992), 70.

3. Joseph Brodsky, "An Immodest Proposal," in *On Grief and Reason* (New York: Farrar, Straus and Giroux, 1997), 208.

4. Gaston Bachelard, *The Poetics of Space* (Boston: Beacon Press, 1969), 46.

5. Daniel Akst, "One Man's Vernacular," *Metropolis* (July 2003): 178.

6. Ibid.

7. Dan Rockhill, introduction to Studio 804.

Projects

Platform House

RURAL PLATTE COUNTY, MISSOURI 2005

The origins for the design are derived from utilitarian buildings of the region and rooted in the economy of the elevated shed.

Designed to replace an existing farmhouse this new building relates to the vernacular tradition of keeping farm buildings elevated above the ground to eliminate moisture and prevent the growth of mold. The new house is elevated above the field and there is a change in height from west to east of over ten feet. A semi detached two-car garage is located alongside. It is placed above the sloping site and faces south to maximize solar gain.

The resultant lightness of form, with its corncrib-like skin of fiber-cement boards, simple rectilinear form, and placement on the grid of the original farmstead relates to both regional farm groupings and the language of modern architecture.

With an overall area of 1,848 square feet the house consists of seven contiguous eleven-foot wide bays each twenty-four feet deep. The entire length of the house is bisected by two continuous tracks that each support two eleven foot wide translucent paneled doors. These enable the owners to change the arrangement of spaces so as to accommodate different activities – exercise routines, office work, host guests and entertain visitors.

The south facade is glazed with continuous floor to ceiling insulated windows. Fabric overhangs shade the openings in the summer and the concrete floors are heated by solar gain during the winter. The exposed concrete slab is also heated with a backup radiant floor heating system. Cross ventilation is an important part of the natural cooling process of the house and this is facilitated by operable windows on the east, west and north sides as well as a ventilation flap on the south side. An outside door, accessible from the living space to the east, leads to an external stair up to a roof terrace with clear views of the skyline of Kansas City.

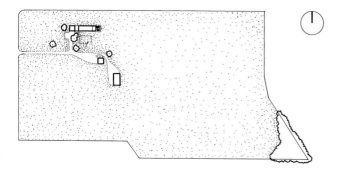

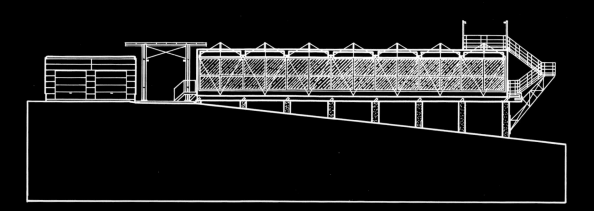

South elevation

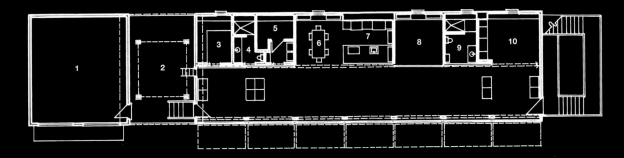

1 Garage	6 Dine
2 Patio	7 Kitchen
3 Office/Bedroom	8 Bedroom/Exercise
4 Guest Bath	9 Master Bath
5 Mechanical/Laundry	10 Master Bedroom

0 5 10 20
FT

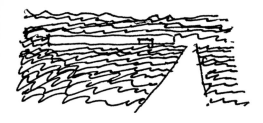

Kansas Longhouse

DOUGLAS COUNTY, KANSAS 2004

The ideas for this house were developed without a specific client, according to our sense of appropriateness for the site and our interest in producing buildings that are comfortable with their rural setting yet contemporary in their execution: a house with proper orientation, a careful selection of materials to promote energy efficiency, a maintenance free exterior and a minimal expenditure for thermal comfort. What evolved was, predictably, a project that relies on a broad exposure on the south elevation and a north face protected by the natural configuration of the topography; a very long form, over 150', with a narrow cross sectional width of 24'.

This eight-acre rural site provides a quick respite into a remarkable landscape that overlooks the floodplain of an adjacent waterway and protects the property from further development. The home site was received in exchange for restoration work performed on the original 400 acre homestead site alongside which included a stone house and three barns.

The process of entry is along a 1,000' long drive, through a field of brome grass, that drops suddenly down to the house and semi-detached garage. A spectacular view of Deer Creek and the agricultural bottomland that borders it unfolds along the approach. The new house, barely visible with its sod roof, is below the brome grass field by a change in height from the north of nearly twelve feet. This affords protection from the Kansas wind and at the same time psychologically transposes visitors into the pristine landscape. A patio, covered by the same roof as the garage and house, separates the two and opens to the southern view. The house includes three bedrooms and two bathrooms with a total area of 2,736 square feet. The plan is open throughout the primary living areas of the kitchen and living room. The large volume of space is interrupted by a core of rooms detached from the outside walls, and is finished in birch-wood. A flexible space, defined for appraisal purposes as two bedrooms, that can be opened easily along their north and south hallway edge is at the heart of the core area.

A tornado shelter doubles as one of two mechanical rooms. Storage needs are addressed with 28 floor-to-ceiling cabinets, providing over 900 cubic feet of storage, that line the entire length of the north wall, interrupted by steel ladders that enable the upper windows to be opened and closed. Cross ventilation is an important part of the natural cooling process of the house. This is supplemented with two whole house fans to assist the process.

The exterior of the house is finished in native limestone, screwed to the captive bolts of a commercial anchoring system, and a light colored corrugated metal siding. All of it is maintenance free. The sod roof, a delightful alternative to asphalt, provides a tremendous increase in the building's thermal performance. Continuing the tradition of Nordic and Native American dwellings, the Longhouse brings together life and nature as well as aesthetics and spirit.

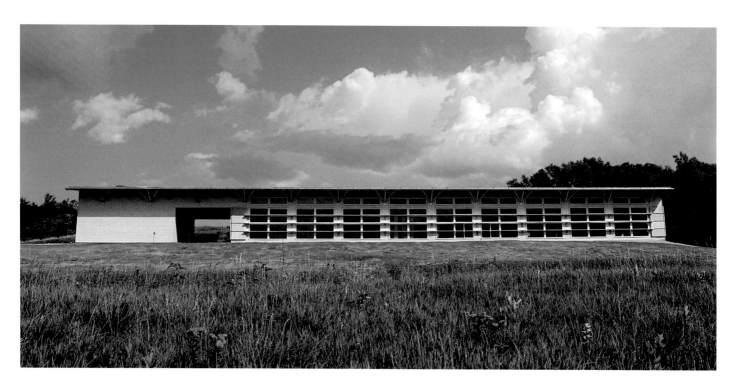

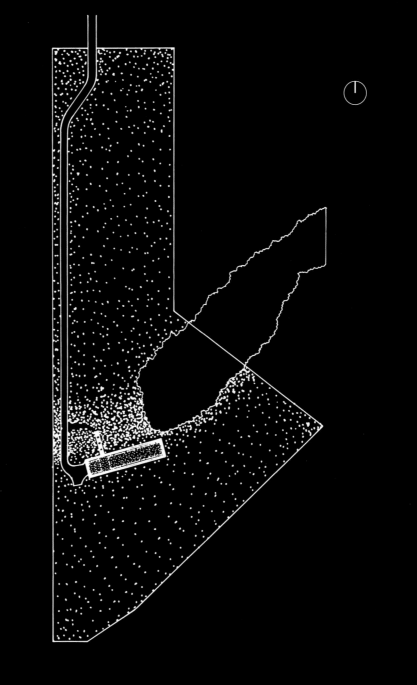

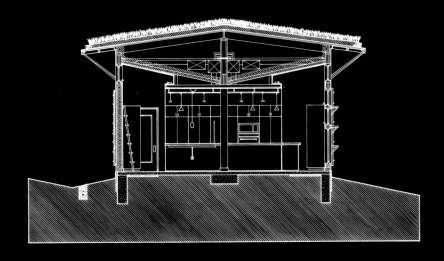

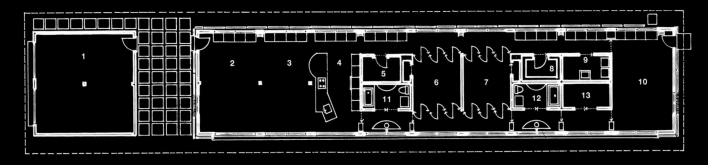

1 Garage   8 Shelter

2 Living   9 Laundry

3 Dine   10 Bedroom

4 Kitchen   11 Bath

5 Mechanical 12 Bath

6 Bedroom   13 Closet

7 Bedroom

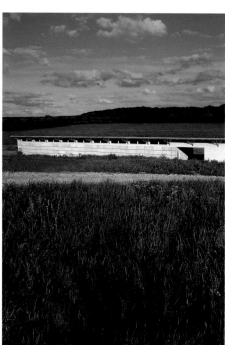

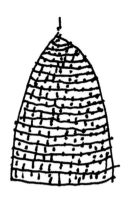

CORE

ST. LOUIS, MISSOURI 2004

CORE is an international advertising and media firm. Recently described in *Graphis* magazine as the *enfant terrible* of the industry, CORE has grown significantly in America and abroad. Having outgrown their existing office space, this design is for a new headquarters and identity to be built at "Grand Center," a newly invigorated music and cultural district on Olive Street in St. Louis.

The design has developed out of the nature of CORE's work and their particular way of working. It is an office with no obvious hierarchy or order. They describe a swarming style of work where people gather at whatever work station is necessary. They also describe themselves as sponges absorbing different information from the world around them and filtering it in their work so as to bring clarity and order to an often complex world of ideas. These factors prompted consideration of the beehive and the sponge as metaphors for the design.

The proposed new building is a simple box with the two public faces, each sheathed in a glass curtain wall that is screened with perforated panels of cement fiberboard. This creates an ever-changing relationship with the world around them. Thus, like a sponge, images of the street and the office are absorbed and emitted depending on the time of day, lighting conditions, individual viewpoints and the ever contingent activities of the office and the street. Inside, the primary workspace is a large two-story volume located in the center of the building. It is the beehive. The space is organized by a series of custom made towers that contain lights and provide power. These serve as reference points around which equipment can be gathered and people swarm.

The entrance is on Olive Street. Two parallel concrete walls support a ramp at the west edge of the site and a staircase at the east. An opening in each wall creates an axis that allows views to the street and across a bridge to the entrance. These rough walls contrast with the smooth, light and transparent character of the glazed elevation. This entry sequence attempts to engage the senses and expand awareness of people working in the building.

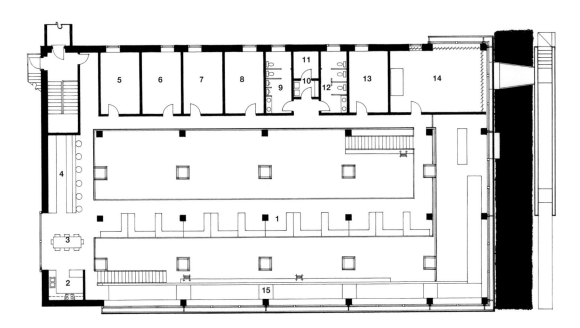

Second Floor

1 Work Stations (Future)
2 Kitchenette
3 Eating Area
4 Bar
5 Library
6 Bedroom (Future)
7 Sound Room (Future)
8 Storage
9 Men's Restroom
10 Laundry
11 Janitor's Closet
12 Women's Restroom
13 Conference (Future)
14 Presentation Room
15 Ramp

```
0    5    10        20
FT
```

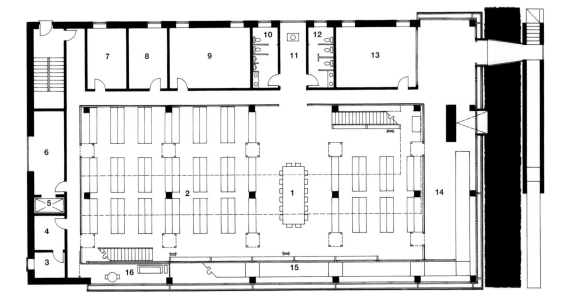

First Floor

1 The Hive
2 The Design Pit
3 Mounting
4 Printing
5 A Hoist for the Basement
6 Storage and Loading Dock
7 Computer Center
8 Fax/Copiers etc.
9 Library
10 Men's Restroom
11 Coffee and Message Walls
12 Women's Restroom
13 Conference Room
14 Gallery
15 Ramp
16 Private Meeting

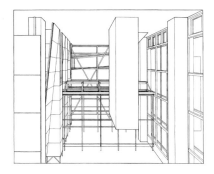

The entire length of the south elevation forms a gallery for the display of CORE's marketing and work by other artists. A constant stream of images projected onto the concrete wall will enable CORE to engage the culture that surrounds them and include people entering. These images will be clearly viewed from the bridge and from certain points in the gallery but will also form dark hazy images through the glass walls and perforated screens.

A ring of circulation will surround the "beehive" while a ramp running from the gallery and along the length of the west elevation connects to a lunchroom and bar on the second floor. The walkway then continues to the east elevation where the support spaces are stacked on both floors. The ring ends at the northeast corner of the building at a conference room that spans over the entry opening with operable louvers opening to the gallery and the street. All rooms and spaces throughout the entire building open immediately to the beehive and an open bridge through the center of the beehive accommodates secondary workspaces.

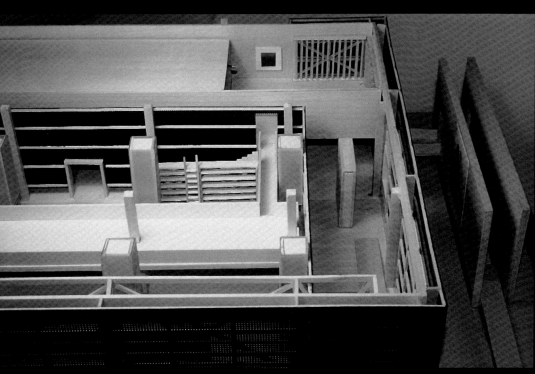

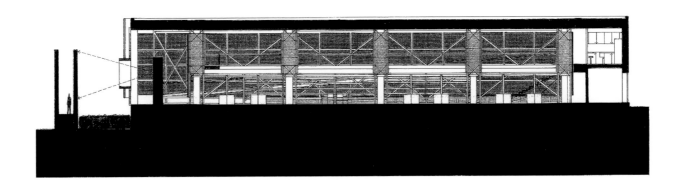

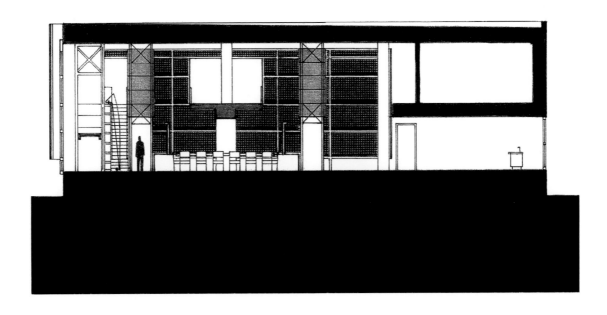

Modern Speak Easy

LAWRENCE, KANSAS 2003

The client for this project, a chef, serves guests from a new kitchen alongside an existing house.

The original stone house, built in the 1870s as a hotel for railroad workers and subsequently used as a boarding house and a brothel, is located at the edge of a working class neighborhood in Lawrence. Situated between an industrial area with manufacturing buildings developed around the railroad and an old but vital residential neighborhood, the house was abandoned for nearly 40 years before being restored in the 1990s, with this latest addition built ten years later.

The project included the renovation of the existing kitchen and bathroom and the design of an addition with a new apartment alongside a detached garden room. Together these buildings define a patio that, in good weather, serves as an outdoor dining area.

The renovated kitchen is separated from the new apartment by a two-storey entry area. This is used as a foyer for the diners and has a restroom for the guests. The ground level of the apartment is a small living room and kitchenette. A narrow staircase leads to the bedroom and bathroom above. A wide bridge at the top of the stairs extends across the entry hall to a library and the bridge doubles as a small reading loft. The kitchen opens onto a patio. It is a small, but important space that mediates between the old house, the kitchen, the main entry and the garden room. This space has views into the garden room as well as the kitchen.

The new addition is clad in translucent tempered glass panels bolted to vertical steel channels. The windows of the apartment

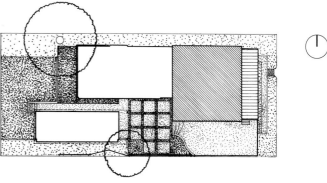

behind this screen allow in air and light. The south elevation consists of a custom-made steel and glass curtain wall. This two-part wall system was designed with the structural tubes supporting the glass loads and resisting wind pressures. Lighter tubes, separated from the structure with a rubber weather break, support the glass. All of the metal work is galvanized. The $3/4$" insulated glass is wet-glazed in place. Brackets on the outside face of the curtain wall support panels of translucent glass that form awnings.

The galvanized steel frames of the garden room are braced with steel diagonals and glazed. A stainless steel mesh drapes from the steel frame between each structural bay and filters the light from the incandescent fixtures above. Between the bays on the south wall there are steel and glass shelves for glassware, wine and the paraphernalia of a meal. These shelves are backed with polycarbonate sheets. The floor is a smooth finished radiant heated concrete slab and the roof of the garden room is grassed.

In the apartment, polycarbonate sheets create dividers which, while providing privacy, also allow light into the small spaces to give them a sense of openness. The bathrooms are finished with aluminum sheet wainscot and angle trim. The sliding doors are custom steel frames, also sheathed in polycarbonate, and hung from exposed tracks. The guest restroom in the entry area revolves around an aluminum-clad shaft that supports custom made shelves and a funnel shaped basin.

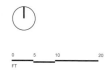

0 5 10 20
FT

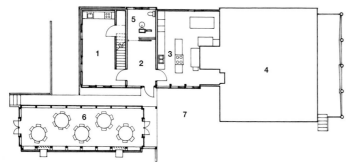

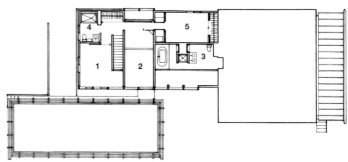

First Floor

1 Living	5 Restroom
2 Foyer	6 Garden Room
3 Kitchen	7 Patio
4 Original House	

Second Floor

1 Bedroom	4 Apartment Bath
2 Open	5 Library
3 House Bath	

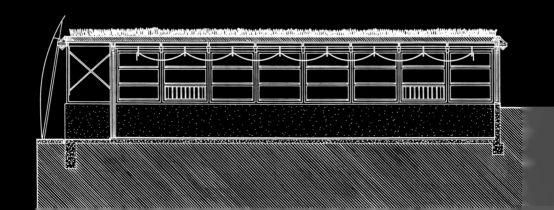

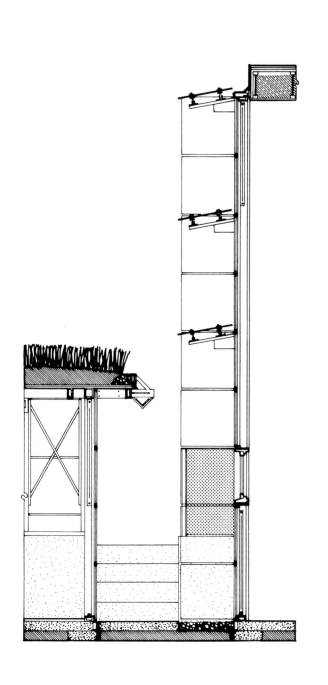

Newton House

DOUGLAS COUNTY, KANSAS 2002

The client, a couple originally from England, purchased a piece of land on the open rolling hills west of Lawrence and have developed a profound appreciation of the landscape in Kansas. Barry Newton is an architect and was interested in integrating design, construction and nature – an interest that led him to consider Rockhill's design-build approach for a new house on the site.

Here, the house is a simple form inspired by the common industrial and agricultural buildings that dot the landscape. They are elementary objects that rest between the earth and the sky, contrasting with both. In this open land the vertical and horizontal are profound. The house is defined by an uninterrupted barrel vault and a continuous *brise-soleil* that runs the length of the building to shield it from the harsh summer sun. Corrugated cement fiberboard is used for siding. The terra cotta red color recalls the block silos of the region.

The single storey house is constructed on a 24' x 110' radiant heated slab and is planned within a series of 10' structural bays. A two bay garage is located at the southern end of the house and a screened porch to the north. The barrel vault roof is expressed along the entire length of the building. From the public entry at the mid-point of the east elevation to the screened porch at the north end, the space is largely open and the roof structure bears on exposed steel trusses. The master bedroom is defined by a curved wall of steel and frosted glass. The steel support structure for the glass is composed of vertical legs that tie into the trusses above and are anchored to the slab below. Glass sheets are treated like shingles, both horizontally and vertically, and screen the view from the hallway while maintaining a sense of openness. Guest bedrooms are

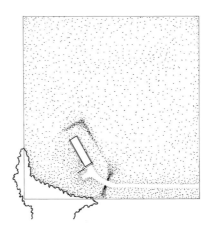

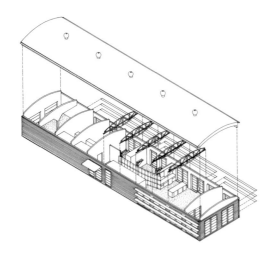

separated from the major living areas. Opposite the bedrooms, on the east side of the hall, are support spaces including a pantry, guest bath, mechanical room and tornado shelter. By making the screen porch an open, three-bay space with large windows lining both walls, the house directly engages the prairie.

All the windows, doors, trusses, and cabinetry were custom fabricated; internally the natural character of the steel has been retained and clear coated. The steel contrasts with the refined quality of the sandblasted glass that has been used as trim for the windows, cabinet doors and drawer fronts, as well as the countertops, shower sides and bathtub surround. The bathtub is a freestanding steel frame that holds four pieces of $1/2$" glass which form the basin. The windows and doors are welded frames composed of galvanized steel angle and tube that are infilled with low-e insulated glass panels. The frames have been set to the outside of the 2x6 walls so the 2" tube perimeter creates a stop for the deep corrugations of the cement fiberboard siding.

1 Garage	5 Kitchen	9 Mechanical
2 Guest Bedrooms	6 Living	10 Laundry
3 Master Bath	7 Porch	11 Guest Bath
4 Master Bedroom	8 Storm Shelter	12 Pantry

0   5   10   20
FT

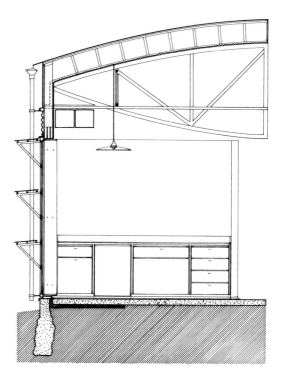

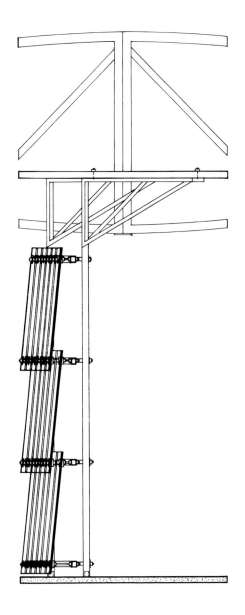

A Wedding on the Kansas Landscape

A Wedding on the Kansas Landscape

DOUGLAS COUNTY, KANSAS 2001

A reception hall and chapel were designed and constructed on an open field adjacent to the childhood home of the bride. Planned to be temporary, these structures existed solely for the event and were then dismantled so that the field could be restored to brome grass. Together, the chapel and hall represent the juxtaposition of life's choices. The chapel, emanating from an inner spirit found in the natural world, is held in marked contrast to the formal, highly rational world imposed by mankind that is embodied in the reception hall.

The chapel was designed to represent the complex order of the natural flora, with its rich symmetry, that blooms from the ground. It was built of felled cottonwood trunks that created an enclosure of dramatically splayed columns. Set in the ground and tied down with thick ropes, this framework formed an "apse" enclosed with a tight weave of limbs and saplings secured to the columns. The altar was a slab of stone slightly raised off the ground. An axis created by a path of maple flooring panels cut from a damaged gym floor extended through the barrel-vaulted pavilion to the apse-like chapel.

The reception pavilion was created by a "lamella arch". This simple form was adopted to create clear spans of generous proportions with common materials. This structure consists of a curved roof framed by a system of interlocking arches. These arches have beveled ends that are drilled and bolted together. Once in place, the horizontal thrust of the arch at the sidewalls is counteracted as the roof acts as a skin. Each member supports the others and shares the load, but no single member is required for the roof to stand. This "lamella arch" was constructed with 2x10s, each slightly less than ten feet long.

The 40'x75' rectangular lamella structure was supported on reused microlam beams and a series of recycled utility poles set into holes dug into the field. These were stabilized with ropes that created diagonal bracing above the arch and were tied to stakes driven into the ground. A cable spanned from each pole to the corresponding column on the opposite side. The cables helped to keep the columns from splaying and also supported lights that illuminated the space. The arch was covered with canvas, which was secured with cap nails to purlins that ran perpendicular to the arch. After the morning dew evaporated, the canvas shrank to a drum-tight translucent shelter. The sidewalls were constructed with salvaged redwood connected to the utility poles with simple steel "forks" that were adjusted to create the gentle curve. Horizontal slats of used flooring gathered these posts and supported the simple burlap that defined the space. A 3,000 square foot x 1½" concrete slab was placed directly on the field and later cut into three-foot squares and removed for other uses.

Materials and Construction

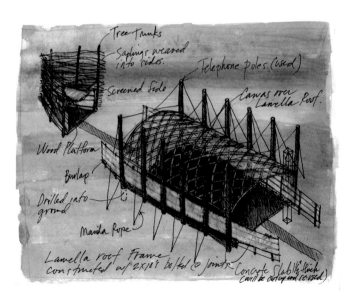

Reception Hall

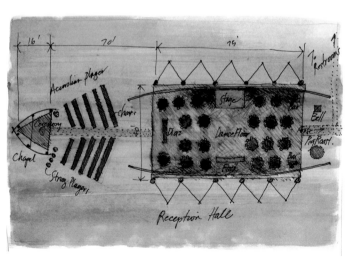

Tombo House

DOUGLAS COUNTY, KANSAS 2000

The client, a professor of business at the University of Kansas, was educated as a cultural anthropologist and has had a life-long interest in Japanese culture. This project is inspired by the *sukiya*, a feature of the traditional farm cottage that realizes the marriage of the house and garden, and the generous *engawa*, or verandah, which engages the space between the two.

In his book, The Poetics of Space, Gaston Bachelard describes the ideal house as one that nurtures the poetic way of life. He suggests that, on one hand, a house should foster a sense of flight, an extension into the surroundings where one engages the natural and cultural world. On the other hand, the house should be a place of retreat, to sleep, to think, and to compose a poetic view of the world.

This house is divided into those realms. Three parallel concrete walls, each 16 feet high, frame the living, kitchen, dining and office spaces that make up the front realm. These walls reach beyond the exterior enclosure to define an entrance, screened porch and gardens. A translucent fiberglass ceiling rises from a center span and overhangs beyond the exterior walls in a gesture to the landscape. To the south the house opens to a meandering clearing in the woods. In the foreground is a water garden collecting the runoff from the roof. In contrast, at the back of the house is a dovetail shaped concrete and wood block that houses the bedrooms and bathrooms. These rooms are focused inward and views are selective. As if tucked in a nest the upper level master bedroom is lit from above – the upper half of the south wall is almost entirely glazed. A small stair leads from the bedroom to a steel grate deck that rests on the concrete walls. At the end of the deck is the "storm shrine," which is reminiscent of the Japanese water shrines and is oriented to offer clear views of the summer storms that characteristically roll across the plains. Throughout the house the interior is divided by prefabricated steel frames that support corrugated fiberglass reinforced plastic panels to create shimmering walls of light with obvious references to the qualities of Japanese *shoji* screens.

The master bathroom is made of concrete. The floor is a smooth concrete slab and the walls are concrete panels. The lavatory is a thin concrete slab notched into the concrete wall and cantilevering into the room where it supports a small under counter bowl. The freestanding custom-made concrete soaking tub is part of a Japanese bathing ritual that is enriched by an east facing floor

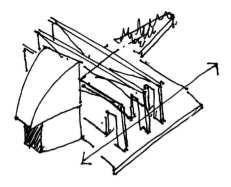

level window that offers morning light and a view to the treetops surrounding the house.

Buddhist art is born from nature and ideas of symmetry played a significant role in the early stages of this design. Buddhists believe that nature seeks symmetry and that the imperfections of life, seen against this demanding search, bring beauty to the world. Early sketches of a wing inspired design prompted the client to point out similarities to the dragonfly – or *tombo* in Japanese. This creature, which holds an important role in Japanese mythology, became another source of inspiration.

The Japanese inspired spaces and forms are quietly anchored to the four universal elements: air, light, water and earth. The house is oriented to take advantage of the prevailing natural resources of its site. The living and dining areas are oriented along the front south wall to benefit from a broad south exposure that maximizes the winter solar gain in the concrete wall and slab floor. The upstairs master bedroom receives sunlight through the translucent plastic panels and is bathed in a glow of light, yet protected from the heat of the summer sun. The dovetail shape of the space and the extended concrete walls minimize the north facing occupied surfaces and help to baffle the cold winds. The south orientation of the building takes advantage of the prevailing spring and summer breezes, which can be brought into the house and help to ventilate the master bedroom windows.

In America concrete has been much maligned; it is seen as little more than a foundation material that is to be covered as quickly as possible. However, the aesthetic qualities and maintenance-free advantages that concrete offers are significant. This client asked for a concrete house and approximately 300 cubic yards of concrete were poured. A series of wood forms of 2x4s and 3/4" plywood were built with block-outs where openings were needed. The lower eight feet of the wall was poured first, as the forms would not have withstood the pressure created by a 16' high pour. This created the entire dragonfly shape. While the concrete cured these forms were then used to support work platforms to construct the upper part of the wall. All the lumber and much of the plywood used to make these forms were later used to frame the building and sheathe the roofs. This project was realized only because of the benefits of the design/build process.

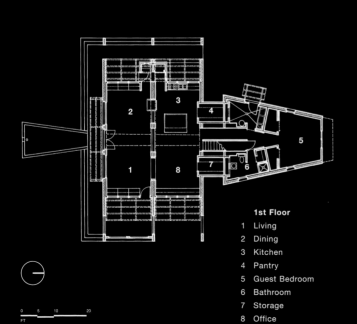

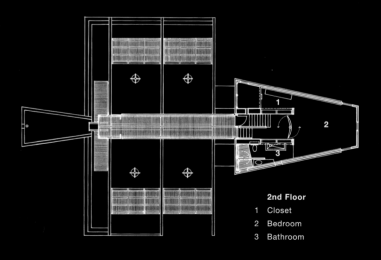

1st Floor
1 Living
2 Dining
3 Kitchen
4 Pantry
5 Guest Bedroom
6 Bathroom
7 Storage
8 Office

2nd Floor
1 Closet
2 Bedroom
3 Bathroom

0   5   10   20
FT

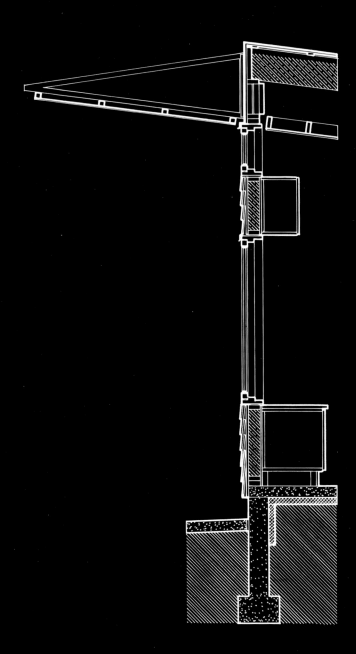

Epard/Porsch House

LAWRENCE, KANSAS 1997-98

The client for this house is a married couple: a grant writer and a software engineer. Their interests include collecting scientific instruments, stargazing, and extensive reading in the natural sciences, art and mythology. Like many of the vernacular buildings of Kansas, this house is composed of multiple simple masonry forms juxtaposed against galvanized steel awnings, decks, bridges and stairs. They are arranged around a garden cut into the site so as to offer a quiet retreat from the noise of a busy neighborhood. The front building, which extends along the street with a gabled roof of Norwegian slate, contains the shared spaces for living, entertaining, cooking and dining. Protruding from the roof is a zinc-clad library that is accessed by a small ladder or hand-lowered rotating stair. The back form is a large rectangular block that is sited away from the street and contains the private spaces of the house. On the second floor there is an exercise room, an office and access to a deck that looks over the sunken garden and the pool. The master bedroom and bath are on the third floor with a quiet office at the most remote and private corner of the building. There is a screened porch adjacent to the bedroom. The forms are bound together by a tower that extends up from a conservatory in the sunken garden with each floor accessed by a bridge that spans over the entry. At the top of the tower is an observatory.

This stair tower anchors the building to the natural world. It also acts as a cooling shaft that has been designed to vent the warm air that rises from the rest of the house.

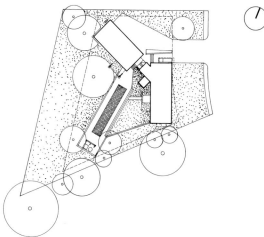

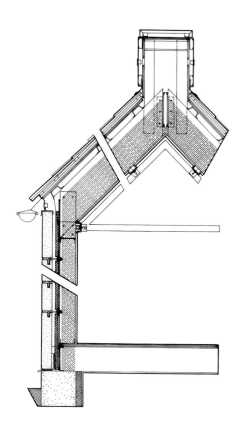

The observatory caps the tower. During the day it offers protection from the sun as well as a view of the entire town and at night, when the cover is lowered with a hand winch, it allows clear views of the sky.

The telescope has been integral to an understanding of the universe since Galileo. Here it is a natural metaphor for a library. A steel and glass structure, resting on a concrete mount and spanning between the trusses along the length of the shaft-like front form, has glass walls that are angled to recall the path of light reflecting through the body of a telescope. It comes to a focal point at the location of a reading chair. A two-story concrete 'telescope mount' surrounds the bathrooms for the first floor and basement and all other spaces revolve around it.

The rotating stair offers an alternative way of reaching the library. It is a sculptural element that hangs above the living room. A tube and pipe structure with birch plywood treads and counterweights of stone scraps, this stair can be raised with ropes and pulleys that are anchored to a frame at the top of the arching guides. The bottom point of each stringer retains an axle for the steel wheels that bear on steel pads set in the floor. The sides of the stair are notched to allow it to nest into the trusses as the entire structure rotates on an upper axle of 1 1/4" steel.

The exterior cladding of the house is a stone veneer cut from large limestone slabs purchased from a regional quarry. The rolling appearance of the coursing made with nine repeating shapes recalls the casual nature of vernacular structures. The library and the top of the tower are sheathed in hand folded sheet zinc – a material that will, over time, weather to a beautiful multi-colored patina.

During the construction of this house 50,000 pounds of steel was hand fabricated to establish a consistent glass and steel vocabulary that is evident throughout the house. All of the components in the stair tower, as well as numerous partitions, cabinet hangers, rolling furniture pieces and the interior sliding doors, adopt the same language. Tempered glass pieces, and occasionally birch plywood sheets, are fixed to these steel frames into a shingle pattern that recalls the exterior windows and doors. The exterior windows and doors, as well as the sunscreen at the library, the observatory cover and the large lean-to structure that supports the second floor deck and the third floor screened porch, were fabricated in steel in sizes that allowed galvanizing and bolting together at the site. In response to one of the client's first requests – to minimize the use of wood – the building makes extensive use of steel.

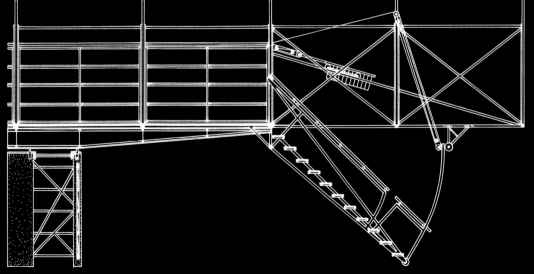

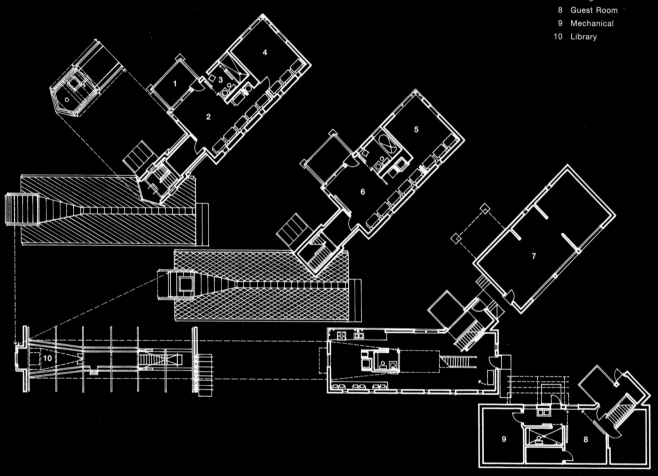

1 Porch
2 Exercise
3 Bathroom
4 Office
5 Office
6 Bedroom
7 Garage
8 Guest Room
9 Mechanical
10 Library

0   5   10   20
FT

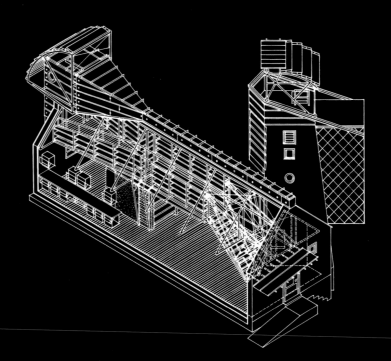

Shimomura/ Davidson-Hues Studio

LAWRENCE, KANSAS 1996

Roger Shimomura is a distinguished professor of art at the University of Kansas, and his wife Janet Davidson-Hues is a respected artist. They produce large-scale pieces that require large open floor space, tall volumes and uninterrupted wall space. In addition they have an extensive art collection to display. The site, located on a busy street on the west side of the city, is long and narrow and slopes twenty feet to the east toward a large pond which is surrounded by other houses. The client wanted the building to act as a screen for traffic noise while allowing the living space to open to the pond. It was also important to avoid direct light on the art collection.

The building was to be used primarily as a studio with adjacent residential space. The budget was similar to that for a typical prefabricated steel shed. The building was designed to be a large, long simple form with few windows. The design proposed a warehouse-like structure with a modular constructional system that utilised rugged industrial materials. The building has a butterfly roof that is consistent along its length and the form is expressed internally. The spine acts as a structural beam as well as a trough to collect rainwater that is directed to the ends of the building where it is discharged from rubber clad "tongues" into steel funnels. The external envelope, designed to reduce maintenance, is a combination of galvanized steel awnings, windows and doors, a corrugated sheet metal roof and 1 1/4" thick precast concrete panels cast on site and fixed to the structural frame.

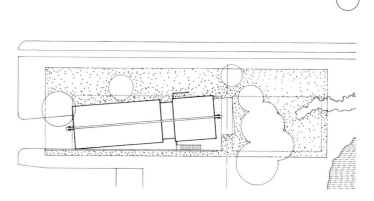

The studio was planned with a garage entrance at the east end. The garage doors rise vertically on external steel frames that are exposed. The main entrance to the house is at the end of a walkway that follows a retaining wall on the north side of the building. It is denoted by a steel awning. The studio is a large open space which is lit by diffused light from high-level windows. The living spaces and offices terminate at the western end of the building in a two-story living room with full-height windows on the northeast corner that frame views of the pond.

The studio floor is a power trowel finished concrete slab that became the work surface for framing the building and forming the concrete cladding panels. These panels are shaped to create a shiplap-like detail. The panels were fabricated using a fiber additive and poured in groups by reusing plywood forms that were leveled on the concrete slab. When they were cured the reinforcing strength of the fiber allowed them to be lifted into place by slipping bolts through the holes and strapping them to the forks of a Bobcat. Once in place, three-inch lag screws were passed through pre-drilled holes into the wood purlins that banded the building. Each panel locks over the one below and the joints were finished with urethane caulk over backer rod.

The building's structural spine is composed of parallel microlams that span from column to column. The bottom of the gutter acts as a frame to prevent them from rotating. The microlams form a seat for 2x12 rafters and span to the 2x6 exterior walls. Each panel included an opening where light enters through a band of glass block at the top of the wall and is reflected into the space by the corrugated metal clad ceiling.

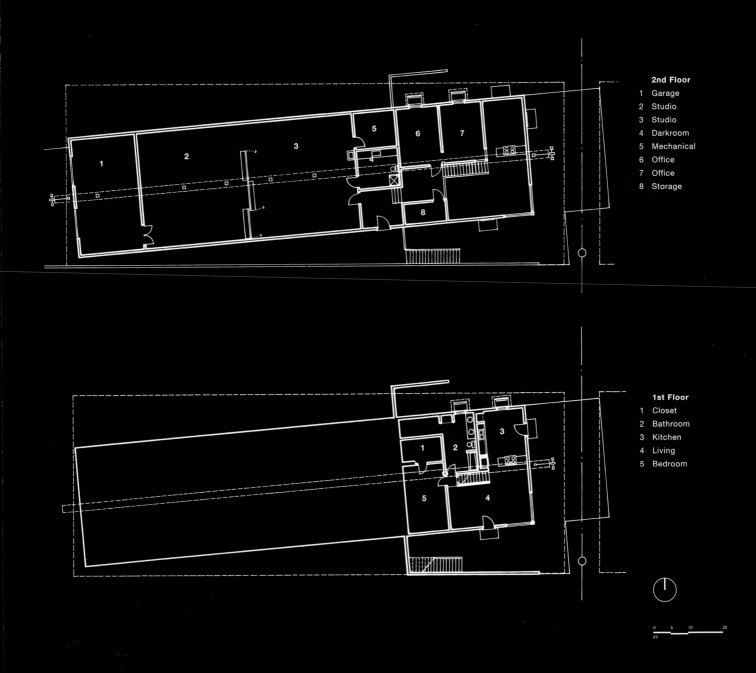

2nd Floor

1 Garage
2 Studio
3 Studio
4 Darkroom
5 Mechanical
6 Office
7 Office
8 Storage

1st Floor

1 Closet
2 Bathroom
3 Kitchen
4 Living
5 Bedroom

0   5   10   20
FT

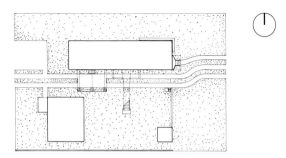

The Dogtrot House on Alabama Street

LAWRENCE, KANSAS 1995

Built on a corner lot, this house is located in an historic neighborhood in Lawrence, Kansas. The site was formerly a bakery and parking lot for the Community Mercantile, a local cooperative grocery that subsequently moved to a larger facility. The store was transformed into a residence and a new house was built on the north edge of the existing parking lot. The bakery, which fronts the alley, was converted into a studio apartment. A small storage shed and low wall along the front of the site gathers the buildings and creates a south facing residential courtyard. The group of buildings is distinctly contemporary while drawing critically from the past. The design builds on the diverse forms, styles and scales of the neighborhood – a mix of grand Victorians, pure white Italianates, and a Wrightian prairie house fronting the garages, carports, storage buildings and fire escapes on the alleys that set the neighborhood apart from the suburbs.

The floor plan is a shotgun, an early American plan type where the rooms are organized in a linear progression. The dining area in this house is glazed in operable steel sash on both the north and south sides to bring light and air to the heart of the house. The living room is open to the front and the kitchen and the bathroom to the back. The bedrooms are reached by a staircase made of steel and mesh that separates the dining and living area. The upper floor is an open volume with rooms defined by frames sheathed in cold rolled sheet steel. Sliding doors hang from exposed wheels while the bathroom stands as an object with the space. A steel deck hung from the side of the building supports a staircase that steps down to the courtyard. All of the buildings were finished with traditional three-coat stucco over super-insulated walls.

The service core forms a framed shape for the entire height of the building. From the basement it vents the furnace and hot water heater. On the main floor it supports the plumbing for the toilet, shower and laundry as well as the kitchen vent. On the upper floor it anchors the bathroom. The core rises above the roof plane in a sheet metal trimmed box that contains all the various flues and vents.

The building plan extends along an east-west axis. The south side is open to the light and the porch structure screens the sun in the summer and reduces the heat gain.

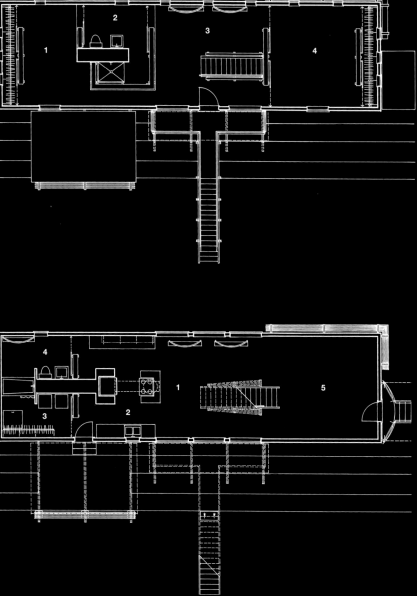

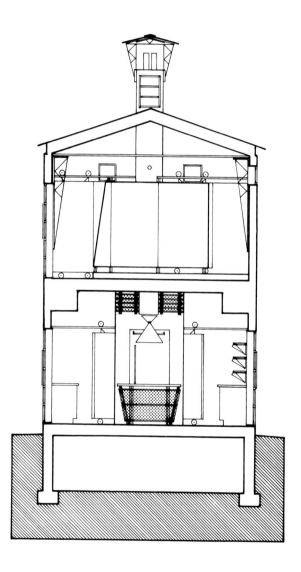

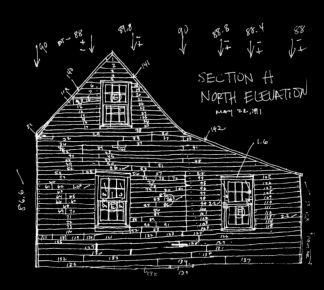

Hobbs Park Memorial

LAWRENCE, KANSAS 2000

This project presented difficult challenges. The building, a small brick and stone structure, played a part in the abolitionist past of Lawrence but was doomed to demolition if it could not be moved. It was built with local limestone and very soft brick set with a lime and sand mortar – as a result the parts of the building were resting in place as much as they were being held in place. To control its natural inclination to implode and find an angle of repose the building was wrapped inside and out with plywood and 2x4 frames that were secured to a welded steel grid. Insulation between the plywood of the frames and the masonry cushioned the materials during the move. The house was put on dollies and slowly towed to Hobbs Park a few blocks away.

Beaumont Water Tower

BEAUMONT, KANSAS 1998

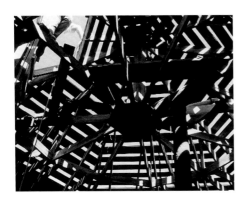

This water tower, built in 1885 in the small town of Beaumont, Kansas at the southern end of the Flint Hills, is thought to be the last tower of its kind in the United States. It served steam locomotives by supplying water for the boilers, as well as for washing the cars, floors and engine houses. Beaumont was a shipping point for cattle destined for eastern markets after fattening on the lush spring pastures in the Flint Hills. The tank is a cypress stave construction bound by steel bands. Large cypress posts, beams and cross braces support the tank that rests upon tapered concrete piers. The restoration consisted of rebuilding the water tank's king post roof truss, repairing the structural members, patching the roof sheathing and replacing the existing cut cedar shingles.

When work started on the water tank it became obvious that the tower had been designed to be full of water and that the shrinkage of the material in the years since it had been empty had caused the tower to slowly dismantle. To meet this unforeseen problem steel and wood braces springing from the newly reinforced king post were used to add interior support and constraint to the perimeter tank. After all the work was complete the tower was sprayed with a sealer to help protect the wood.

Epoxy resins were used to repair the failing wood. In the case of the structural members, many of the cypress posts, beams and diagonals had deteriorated, either at the exposed ends or joints. The soft lumber was saturated with liquid epoxy and then shapeable putty inserted, carved to shape and stained to match the aged cypress. Epoxy was also injected into the cracked and crumbling concrete piers that were patched and coated with an opaque concrete sealer. The interior of the tank was cleaned and almost a foot of debris removed before its side walls were re-anchored to the floor. The entire roof frame was sistered with treated lumber to give support to its hexagonal roof.

Runnymede Church

HARPER, KANSAS 1996

This church was originally built in 1890 as part of Runnymede, Kansas – an English settlement for second sons who were expected to make their fortunes on the plains of America after the first sons had inherited the family wealth. At its peak the town had a racetrack, playing fields, hotels and this church. The community quickly failed but the church was salvaged. In 1893 it was relocated to Harper, Kansas with its original finishes, stained glass and baptismal font. The work on this project was marked by the discovery of a time capsule nested meticulously in a hollowed out corner stone. The lead boxes were carefully cut open to find that they contained many papers: including newspapers, stamps from the Colombian Exposition of 1893 and the original charter of the church – almost all preserved and in good condition.

Constitution Hall

LECOMPTON, KANSAS
1990, 1995

Built as a land office in 1856, Constitution Hall is one of the oldest wood frame structures in Kansas still standing. In the same year that it was built the pro-slavery Lecompton Constitution for Kansas was passed in the building and as both pro- and anti-slavery forces clashed over the formation of that constitution, so the events that preceded this coined the term "Bleeding Kansas." Over the past 135 years the building had many different uses, including offices, a mortuary, a carriage shop, a hotel, apartments and a fraternal lodge. Despite hard use and these changes, the building remained surprisingly unaltered and many of the original materials were still intact. The original wide plank flooring was still under the latter-day floorboards and the building still rested on timber sills milled and shaped from regional cottonwood. In 1986 the building was purchased by the State of Kansas and is now a State Historical Site museum dedicated to this era of the region's history.

The first phase of the restoration was to stabilize the building's structure. The building was lifted off its severely deteriorated stone foundation and a series of 60' long, 12" deep steel beams inserted through the building to lift it from beneath the second floor as the first floor was deemed too flimsy to enable a safe lift. Before removing the flooring and joists each piece was labeled and documented to assure accuracy when the building was re-assembled. The stone foundation was photographed and diagrammed. Each stone was numbered as it was removed and laid out on the ground and a new concrete footing was poured. Each course of stone was then reset in its original location based upon precise elevations taken before the wall was dismantled. The existing cottonwood sills were repaired and, where necessary, replacements were milled by a local sawyer. The intricate joinery of the originals was matched by using chisels and augers in making new.

In a second phase of work Constitution Hall was completely fitted out as a museum with a shop, restrooms and a curator's office.

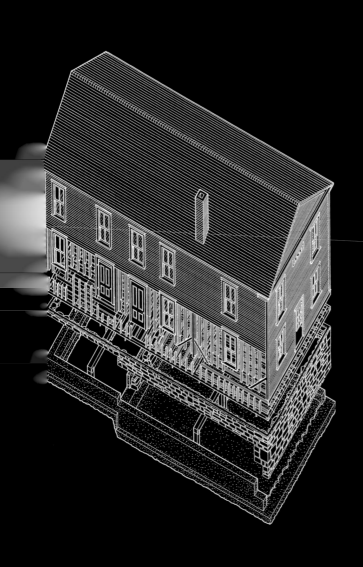

Fort Hays Blockhouse

HAYS, KANSAS 1993

Old Fort Hays was established in the 1860s to protect railroad workers and provide supplies to the forts in western Kansas that were not yet serviced by the railroad. Its history includes visits by George Armstrong Custer, Wild Bill Hickok and Buffalo Bill. Of the original stone buildings that comprised the Fort, the blockhouse has survived and remains largely unchanged. It was built as a defensive strongpoint with gun slots and a reinforced second floor to hold army howitzers.

Severe damp for more than one hundred years rising along the base course of stone had caused the building's previous owners to concrete over this grade line of stone. Also, over the last 140 years the fort's soft native limestone walls have been carved with names, hometowns and personal messages. Many of these date back to the early days of the fort and are now historic artifacts. These were the primary reasons the Kansas State Historical Society wanted to preserve every stone possible. The building was thoroughly documented and stone deemed salvageable was repaired with liquid epoxy that was pumped into the cracks using a syringe. The epoxy absorbed into the porous stone and adhered the sides. Despite the efforts to keep as much of the original stone as possible over 700 cubic feet of new limestone was cut from the same quarry used by the soldiers in the 1860s. The new limestone was brought back to the blockhouse where wedges and hammers similar to those used in the 1860s were used to dress each piece of stone to the required size and match the existing chisel markings.

Cottonwood Ranch

STUDLEY, KANSAS 1992-1993

The Pratt family homesteaded Cottonwood Ranch in the 1870s. They were comparatively wealthy and the ranch quickly became a center of sheep ranching, entertainment and leisure. Tom Pratt borrowed money from other English families and lent it, with interest, to his fellow settlers. This venture, and the success of the ranch, helped finance the expansion of the homestead. What started as a small stone building with a sod roof soon had a wood roof and two wings as well as numerous outbuildings — most of which stand today. The Pratt family lived at the ranch for more than 100 years until the Kansas State Historical Society purchased it in 1982. While inventorying the outbuildings during its transfer to the state it was discovered that Tom Pratt had been an early advocate of photography and left behind hundreds of glass negatives of the ranch and life in the region. This invaluable asset propelled the project to the forefront of the state's historical priorities. The restoration work was done in two phases. First, the Pratt family house was restored and several years later, the outbuildings, gates and corrals that form the ranch were subsequently restored. Cottonwood Ranch is now a unique collection of buildings and artifacts with the long-term goal of becoming a living history ranch that recreates the 19th century life documented in Tom Pratt's photos.

Rebuilding Cottonwood Ranch's masonry outbuildings — including the bunkhouse, stables, shearing shed and corral — was dramatic. The roof frames and their interior structure — all over one hundred years old — were to remain in place, temporality supported while each stone was removed, cleaned and re-laid in exactly the same location.

The house was to be returned to the splendor of its earlier days and this involved removing and re-laying any bulging or loose stones and tuck-pointing the walls. The cedar shingle roof was replaced and new half round gutter hung. Stainless steel liners were inserted into the chimneys and brick re-laid from the roofline up. The studs at the base of the wood bay windows were repaired and all of the windows and doors were returned to operable condition. Wallpaper was removed and cracked or collapsed walls were repaired with new three-coat plaster. The house's living room had an ornate pressed tin ceiling and paint was stripped from every seam and fold before the ceiling was sprayed with a new coat.

Hollenberg Pony Express Station

NEAR HOLLENBERG,
KANSAS 1991

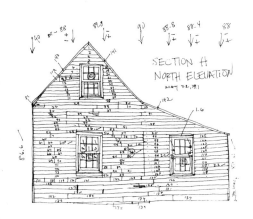

The Hollenberg Station, built in 1861, is the only intact and relatively unaltered station that remains from the colorful history of the Pony Express. Consisting of six buildings built over the years and united with walnut siding, the station is a textbook of historic building traditions including log construction, masonry, timber and light frame. This project aimed to accurately restore the building's foundation, stabilize the deteriorated frame, replace most of the siding with new walnut, roof it with new cedar shingles and make extensive repairs to all doors, windows, plaster and floors using historic guidelines set forth by the Department of the Interior and referred to universally as the Standards for the Rehabilitation of Historic Structures.

Like Constitution Hall this building was lifted off of its foundation. In this case it also needed to be moved to the side in order to provide access for a two-week archeological dig. The six buildings were gathered together and lifted against a frame that was added to the building to avoid lifting against original material. Before the lift all the floors were removed revealing an early form of on-grade construction. Logs of either red elm or walnut were placed directly on the leveled ground and flooring was nailed to their topsides creating a very quick and surprisingly long lasting floor assembly.

The existing stone foundation, which barely went beneath the surface of the ground, was dismantled and each stone was documented and removed. A new footing was poured and the foundation relayed according to the documentation so as to meet the unique form of the building. The timber sills came in a variety of shapes, species and conditions. If the existing material was at all salvageable it was repaired with epoxy in accordance with recommended standards. Already a dozen species of wood had been used including red oak sills, walnut siding and hickory rafters. Each was considered with a clear understanding of its individual capacity to resist rot and provide structural strength. Before any of the walnut siding was removed, the building was thoroughly documented and each piece of siding was numbered. The drawings and old photos of the building gathered by the Kansas State Historical Society were used to re-side the building using replacement walnut that matched saw blade marks and mill marks as accurately as possible.

Studio 804

Studio 804 is a graduate design build project at the University of Kansas that is carried out annually by students directed by Dan Rockhill.

The work of Studio 804 is an opportunity to explore concepts and issues like those that confront professionals. There is a commitment to the exploration of ideas within the confines of the contemporary world. We believe in making environments that are accessible to anyone, not only in a physical sense, but also monetary. We believe that creative young minds can make a difference in the affordable housing community and that we can dispel the notion that architects only provide services to the advantaged. All design and construction is performed by the students, with the exception of the licensed trades; electric, plumbing and heating/air conditioning. Students build formwork, do flatwork, build cabinets, lay flooring, frame walls, cut rafters, run membrane roofing, make concrete countertops, and recycle materials. It is a fully involved hands-on experience where gender and experience have little bearing on participation. To date, seven houses have been designed and built.

Shawnee Road House

KANSAS CITY, KANSAS 2005

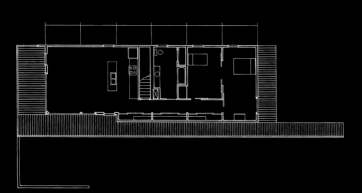

This Studio 804 house responds to lessons learned from the earlier house designs and in particular the sixth project – the first to explore prefabrication. The client, City Vision Ministries, expanded the programmatic requirements of this latest project to include an attached garage and an unfinished third bedroom. These reflect real estate market considerations with a view to improving the appraisal rates.

The site lent itself to placing the garage on the lower level with access from a drive which wraps around from the street. This resulted in a fire separation requirement that was satisfied by adding the optional third bedroom in the remaining basement space with a laundry room in between.

The use of horizontal channel glass, recycled from a Kansas City museum project, adds a beautiful quality of light in the living space. Recycled aluminum is used on the exterior face of the recessed window areas. The exterior is clad in natural cypress and internal finishes include recycled maple flooring and a custom maple storage wall.

Lloyd Street House

KANSAS CITY, KANSAS 2004

This is the sixth house designed in Studio 804 and the first to be prefabricated. A flexible floor plan was devised and tailored to suit our client's specific requirements for the building and site available. The house, designed as five transportable 12'x20' modules, was built in a warehouse in Lawrence and trucked to the site in Kansas City where the modules were set in place with a crane. The project was the result of a development partnership with City Vision Ministries, the Unified Government of Wyandotte County and the Rosedale Development Association. The partnership placed the physical and financial groundwork to transform a former neighborhood dump site into a viable building lot. Everyone involved supported the concept that modern dwellings mixed into the older urban fabric can serve as a stimulus for re-energizing older neighborhoods.

The units were set, in one day, on a full concrete basement. The outside of the building is finished in Brazilian hardwood. The garage, which was built in place, is finished in the same material. The interior is built around a central core that includes all of the utilities and is finished in recycled aluminum sheet. Bamboo is the floor finish throughout the interior.

0   5   10   20
FT

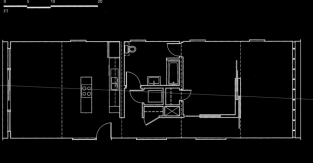

Atherton Court House

LAWRENCE, KANSAS 2003

The fifth house provides three bedrooms and two bathrooms. The site made it possible for the house to be broken down into two simple forms with the kitchen as a hub linking the two. The garage has been planned so as to provide a protected semi-private exterior space off the kitchen. By taking advantage of a south facing site the use of passive solar energy has been maximised. The broad south exposure of each form is faced with glazing created from industrial windows that were rescued from a demolition site. In order to hold the heat from the winter sun, significant thermal mass has been introduced in the form of water tubes that will emit warmth to the interior long after the sun sets. Cellular window shades keep the heat in at night. Carefully calculated overhangs and a louvered screen protect the elevation from overheating in the summer when the sun is high and a light shelf along the upper edge bounces daylight back into the house. The entire roof floats above the form on "super-glass," a recent development in glass technology that has an "R" value of 13 – equivalent to that of an insulated wall.

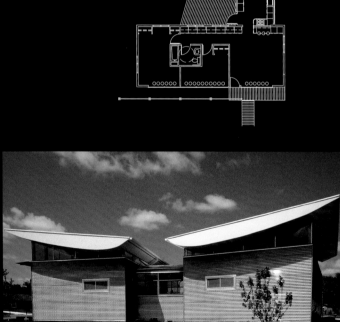

0 5 10 20
FT

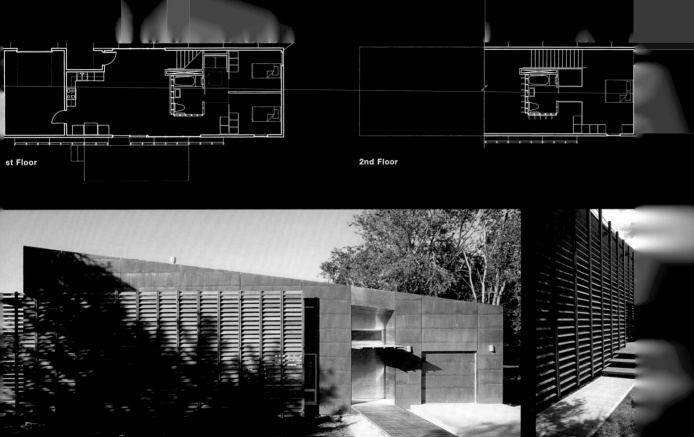

st Floor

2nd Floor

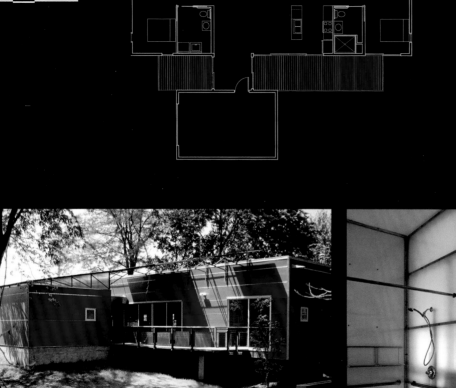

Postscript

TOD WILLIAMS

To think of Dan Rockhill as merely an architect working on the plains in Kansas is to underestimate him, the work and the power of architecture. Work well done is work well done *anywhere*. Architecture well done knows no boundaries yet each place in the world brings its own challenges. Rockhill has practiced primarily within the small community of Lawrence in eastern Kansas. From afar, whether New York, Buffalo or Helsinki, one might imagine the constraints of this apparently distant and isolated community as being different from our own. Of course they may be, but the creative search is the same. To imagine that life for Rockhill is more, or less, difficult than for colleagues elsewhere is to unnecessarily elevate or disparage one while ignoring the other.

Like all architects of quality Rockhill deserves recognition. His socially conscious projects, designed and built with students, have been significant not only for those students but also for faculty, homeowners, city fathers and the wider community. They present an admirable educational model for us all. His energy and hands-on design bring to mind Sam Mockbee, Will Bruder and Rick Joy. In other ways it might also remind us of the great focused talents of Peter Zumthor and Glenn Murcutt. The work is visceral rather than cerebral. Yet Rockhill is not an anti-intellectual: it is that his enormous energy and talents have been located in and committed to the making of meaningful marks in the landscape of Kansas.

Several years ago I visited some of Rockhill's buildings. The work was engaging, not perfect, but with a fresh, passionate and optimistic quality that also captured the spirit of those who are part of his creative search. I returned to New York excited to know that this search exists – not just in Kansas – but that it exists and is real.

Looking at his work today I feel that the investigations have gone deeper, the work is better, that there is still an extraordinary joy in the making and that references to particular forms and expressions are more subtle. The work is less self-conscious, has a more deeply rooted sense of confidence and, as a result, is more strongly connected to the landscape of Kansas and the land in general.

This seems like an appropriate moment then to remind ourselves that good work and the passionate, creative search for truth is ours if we are not afraid to be a part of the world that surrounds us.

Appendices

Awards

2005

Boston Society of Architects Award, "In The Pursuit of Housing".

2004

Architecture Magazine's Home of the Year Award, Modular 1 House.

Wood Design & Building Magazine, **Wood Design Award,** Modular 1 House.

2003

Graham Foundation for Advanced Studies in the Fine Arts, Grant recipient, The Work Of Rockhill and Associates, support for publication.

Graham Foundation for Advanced Studies in the Fine Arts, Grant recipient, Contemporary Interpretations of the Kansas Vernacular Landscape: The Work Of Rockhill and Associates, support for exhibition.

NCARB Prize for Creative Integration of Practice and Education in the Academy.

Bank of America Design Award Winner, HOME House Project.

2002

Wood Design & Building Magazine, **Wood Design Award,** Kansas Plains Wedding Chapel and Pavilion.

Design Build Institute of America, Distinguished Leadership Award.

Dwell Magazine, **Modernist Award,** Anniversary Issue.

Dragonfly House Award, American Concrete Institute, Kansas chapter.

2001

Kemper Fellow, Distinguished Teaching Award, University of Kansas.

Excellence in Teaching Award, KU Center for Teaching Excellence.

First Place Award, Association of Collegiate School of Architecture (ACSA) Steel Tube Competition, Studio 804, 1603 Random Road.

Third Place, David Award. Archeworks, Chicago, "Excellence in Design for People with Disabilities," Studio 804, 1603 Random Road.

First Place, "Design with Memory," International competition for sustainable design, 1603 Random Road.

Finalist, World Architecture Awards, Studio 804, 216 Alabama.

Judges Award, RADA 2001, Studio 804, 216 Alabama, *Residential Architect,* Professional Competition.

Building Stone Institute, "Tucker Architectural Award."

2000

Design Matters; Best Practices in Affordable Housing, City Design Center, University of Illinois, Chicago, Studio 804, 216 Alabama.

Livable Communities Award, The American Institute of Architects, Studio 804, 216 Alabama.

Grand Prize, Residential Architect, Affordable Housing Competition, Studio 804, 1144 Pennsylvania.

First Place Award, ACSA Steel Tube Competition, Studio 804, 216 Alabama, May.

Affordable Housing Award, Federal Home Loan Bank, Studio 804, 922 and 1144 Pennsylvania and 216 Alabama.

1999

Honorable Mention, ACSA, Steel Tube Competition, Studio 804, 1144 Pennsylvania.

1998

Global Home Award, Structural Board Association, Studio 804, 922 Pennsylvania.

1997

First Place Award, ACSA Steel Tube Competition, Studio 804, Building Yard Cover for Marvin Hall.

1996

Education Honors Award, American Institute of Architects, Studio 603, Introductory Graduate Studio.

1991

Bradley Teaching Award, School of Architecture, University of Kansas.

Design Award, ACSA, Teaching and Practice.

1989

Education Honors Award, American Institute of Architects, ARCH 623, Building Practicum.

Historic Preservation Alliance Awards for 12 projects.

Lawrence Arts Commission Award, S.E.W.S. House.

American Concrete Institute, Gridley Dome.

Publications

Marrerios, Sabina. "Glass Design,"
Fusion Publishing, Stuttgart, Germany

Jacobs, Karrie. "The Perfect $100,000 House."
Viking Press (2006).

Kurlander, Caren. "Platform House."
Western Interiors (2006).

Lawrence, Robyn. "Ten Best Green Firms 2005,"
Natural Home & Garden.

Oblenski, Kira. "Bold," *Goodhouse Cheaphouse*
(Sept. 2005): 58-64.

Sparkes, Ken. "Prefab." *Spaces Magazine*,
London, UK (Sept. 2005).

"62 Reasons To Love Your Country,"
Gentleman's Quarterly (July 2005).

Chapin, Lauren. "Home Sweet Restaurant."
Kansas City Star (June 15, 2005).

Bell, Jonathan. "Modular 2." *21st Century Office*,
London, UK (2005).

Bouknight, Joanne Kellar. "Style and Delight on a
Budget." *Celebrating the American Home*,
Taunton Press/AIA (2005): 152-155.

Ebong, Ima. "Studio 804." *Kit Homes Modern*,
Collins (2005).

"Kansas Longhouse." *Sustainable Architecture
in the USA.* Barcelona: Links Publishing (2005).

Paredes, Cristina. "Rural Missouri House."
Architectural Inspirations, Loft Publications,
Barcelona (2005).

Pollzzie, Brian. "Prairie Progressive." *Breathe*,
(May/June 2005): 40-41.

Wagner, Andrew. "Dan Rockhill on Studio 804."
Dwell (May 2005): 126-7.

Suning, Fan. "Modular I House." *Tsinghua University
Architecture Publications.* Beijing (April 2005).

Lecuyer, Annette. "Studio 804." *DeArchitect*
The Hague (April 2005).

Nieand, Jane. "Craftsmanship Awards."
Iowa Architect (March 2005).

Lawrence, Robyn. "Longhouse on the Prairie."
Natural Home & Garden (March 2005): 54-59.

Vassallo, Marc. "Longhouse." *The Barefoot Home.*
Taunton Press (2005).

Hill, Steven. "Mod Squad." *Kansas Alumni* 1
(2005): 57-8.

Lees, Misty. "It Isn't Easy." *KC Magazine*
(Jan. 2005): 72-9.

Brown, David. "2003 House." *The Home House
Project* (Dec. 2004): 74-5.

Rockhill, Dan. "The Deck Upstairs." *Roofing,
Flashing, and Water* (Dec. 2004).

"Home of the Year Award; First Award, Modular 1
House, Studio 804." *Architecture* (Nov. 2004): 38-43.

Boschetti, Joe. "E/P House," *Contemporary
Houses*, Australia (2004).

Iano, Joe. "Evocative Wood Shell." *Iano's Backfill*,
Wood Light Frame Construction, 2004.

Jacobs, Peter. "The Newton House." *Abstract; The
Best of International Architecture & Design*, 34-8.
Brussels, 2004.

Landon, Jan. "Rockhill's World." *Lawrence
Magazine* (Winter 2004): 42-7.

Hoedel, Cindy. "Q+A." *Kansas City Star*
(Oct. 31, 2004): E2.

Maynard, Nigel. "Glory Glaze." *Residential
Architect* (Oct. 2004): 119.

Bonet, Llorenc. "E/P House, Newton's."
Contemporary Houses (Oct. 2004).

"Modular 1 House." *Wood Design and Building*
(Autumn 2004).

Grady, Mark. "Snapshot: Dan Rockhill."
The Zweigletter (Aug. 2004).

Yang, Andrew. "Familiarity With Blueprint And
Hammer Come in Handy." *The New York Times*
(Aug. 5, 2004).

Greenberg, Randi. "Newton House." *Architectural
Record* (July 2004).

Darr, Andrea. "The Great Room Divide." *KCHG*
(June 2004): 92-5.

Cox, Chelsie. "A Reflection of Taste." *Do!* (June 2004).

Sylvester, Michael. "Modular I House."
Fabprefab.com (Spring 2004).

Bochetti, Joe. "Tombo House." *Water Spaces.*
Australia, 2004.

Bussel, Abby. "Prefabricated Modular House."
Architecture (April 2004).

Hutchins, Shelly. "Bathed in Light." *Custom Home*
(March 2004).

Hill, John. "Reality Dose On the Prairie."
Ten by Ten 3, no. 2 (2004): 40-4.

Darr, Andrea. "Terrace House," *KCHG*
(March 2004).

Hutchins, Shelly. "Movable Walls."
Custom Home (March 2004).

Bochetti, Joe. "Speak Easy." *Interiors USA and
Canada.* Australia, 2004.

Lind, Diana. "An Exercise in Poetry and Parenting,"
Architectural Record, (Dec. 2003): 53.

Behunek, Sara. "Shelter from the Sun." *KCHG*
(Dec. 2003): 78-83.

Kodis, Michelle. "Newton House."
Blueprint Affordable (Dec. 2003): 142-55.

"Awards Issue." *Texas Architect* (2003).

Castillo, Encarla. "Shimomura/DH."
Maximinimalism. Spain, 2003.

Mahoney, Lindsey. "… the Architect." *306090*
(Sept. 2003).

Darr, Andrea. "Flight of the Dragonfly." *KCHG*
(Sept. 2003): 86-9.

Hill, Steven. "Space To Learn." *Kansas Alumni* 4
(2003): 16-21.

McGraw, Hesse. "Studio 804." *Review* (2003): 7.

Gabbard, Todd. "Chrysalis." *Crit* 57: 44.

Groves, Shanna. "Salvage Materials." *KC Star*,
(August 2003).

Paul, Steve. "Hammer and Lesson." *Kansas City Star* (April 22, 2003): E1.

Rockhill, Dan. "A House With Wings." *Small Homes*, 88-95. 2003.

"Great Escape," *Custom Home* (Jan./Feb. 2003): 42.

The Best of Fine Homebuilding [CD-ROM]. Taunton Press, 2002.

Pearson, Jason. "Studio 804." *University-Community Design Partnerships: Innovations in Practice*, 97-106. National Endowment for the Arts, 2002.

"A Wedding on the Kansas Landscape." *Wood Design and Building* 21 (Autumn 2002): 18-19.

Arieff, Alison. "Meet Our Nice Modernists." *Dwell* 10 (2002): 16.

McGraw, Hesse. "Residential Design for a New Cultural Paradigm." *Review* (July/Aug. 2002): 50-5.

Akst, Daniel. "One Man's Vernacular." *Metropolis* (July 2002): 136-9.

"Rockhill's Studio 804." metropolismag.com (July 2002).

Trulove, James. "Timber Tower." *Private Towers*, 176-89. 2002.

Rockhill, Dan. "…Concrete," *Fine Homebuilding*, (March 2002): 102-103.

Archer-Barnstone, Deborah. "Building Designs for Living: Studio 804, University of Kansas." *Journal of Architectural Education* (Feb. 2002): 186-93.

Knecht, Barbara. "Plastics Finally Get Respect." *Architectural Record* (Dec. 2001): 107-12.

Jiricna, Eva. "Epard/Porsch Moving Stair." *Staircases* (Dec. 2001).

Maynard, Nigel. "Q+A." *Residential Architect* (Nov./Dec. 2001).

Weber, Cheryl. "Pro Bono's Pros and Cons." *Residential Architect* (Nov./Dec. 2001): 28-36.

Arieff, Allison. "701 Alabama." *Dwell* (Oct. 2001).

Rockhill, Dan, and David Sain. "Building Old Building New." *Embattled Lawrence*. 2001.

"Studio 804, 216 Alabama." *World Architecture* (April 2001).

Kim, Il. "922 Missouri." *New American House Additions* (2001).

Truelove, James. "Mackie House." *Hot Dirt, Cool Straw* (2001): 110-16.

Rockhill, Dan. "The Dragonfly House." *Fine Homebuilding* (Summer 2001).

Truelove, James. "Epard/Porsch House." *New American House* 3 (2001): 42-52.

"Tombo House." *Roadmap to Green Buildings* (Dec. 2000).

Knox, Mathew. "Lawrence House." *AR34, The AIA Kansas Magazine* (Sept. 2000): 12-16.

Drape, Trisha. "Wings of a Home." *Kansas City Star* (Sept. 10, 2000): 31-9.

Sullwood, Tracy. "Modern Master." *Kansas City Star* (Aug. 27, 2000): 17-19.

Hill, Steven. "Vernacular Modernism." *Notre Dame Magazine* (Summer 2000): 32-3.

William Stephan. "Design Lab Mutants." *New York Times* (May 11, 2000): F6.

O'Brien, Tom. "Student Architects Create Housing." *Fine Homebuilding* (March 2000): 54.

Moonan, Wendy. "This is Kansas." *House and Garden* (Jan. 2000): 136-41.

Bickford, Charles. "Tools on Board." *Fine Homebuilding* (Jan. 2000): 92-7.

"Salvage House." *Home* (Sept. 1999): 130-3.

"Case Studies." *Roadmap to Green Buildings* (July 1999).

Toplin, Jim. "Salvage Yard Vernacular." *The New Cottage Home*, 156-61. 1999.

"Epard/Porsch House." OZ (Kansas State University, College of Architecture) 21 (1999): 4-9.

Arcidi, Philip. "Kansas Combine." *Architecture* (Dec. 1998): 60-5.

Lesnikowski, Wojciech. "DWA DOMY." *Architectura & Bizines* (Warsaw) (June 1998): 27-31.

"Learn by Doing." *Residential Architect* (May 1998): 8.

Paul, Donna. "Homes of Metal." *New York Times* (May 14, 1998).

Dommer, Dennis. "Building Memory." *The Structuralist* 37/38 (1997/98): 32.

Bilello, Joe. "Hands on Learning." *Architecture* (Nov. 1996): 100-11.

Moonan, Wendy. "Making Architecture Happen," *Architectural Record* (April 1995): 26-31.

Cantrell, Scott. "Shotgun House." *Kansas City Star* (Dec. 1994): 1-3.

Dietsch, Debora. "Design Backlash." *Architecture* (July 1993): 15.

Trelstad, Julie. "Stick and Steel." *Progressive Architecture* (Aug. 1992): 58-60.

"Compact Passive Solar." *Small Houses* (1992): 91-5.

Cantrell, Scott. "Farmhouse Makeover." *Kansas City Star* (Sept. 1991).

Landecker, Heidi. "Recycling Redux." *Architecture* (May 1991): 90-5.

"Stemwall Foundation." *Foundations and Masonry* (1990): 20-5.

Majur, Janet. "The Restorationists." *Preservation News* (Spring 1990): 12-18.

Rockhill, Dan. "Levels." *Fine Homebuilding* (March 1990): 42-5.

"Foundations." *Building with Concrete, Brick and Stone* (1989): 24-9.

"Concrete Belvedere." *Building with Concrete, Brick and Stone* (1989): 80-5.

Rockhill, Dan. "The Monthly Design Column." *Journal of Light Construction* (Jan.-Dec. 1989).

Rockhill, Dan. "Structural Restoration with Epoxy Resins." *The Association for Preservation Technology* Journal 3 (1988): 29-34.

Rockhill, Dan. "Tudor Hardtop." *Fine Homebuilding* (June 1988): 56-60.

Rockhill, Dan. "One Stop Shop." *Fine Homebuilding* (Spring 1988): 20-6.

Rockhill, Dan. "Stemwall Foundations." *Fine Homebuilding* (March 1988): 32-7.

Rockhill, Dan. "Architecture Model." *Fine Homebuilding* (Sept. 1987): 32-6.

Rockhill, Dan. "Review: Sun, Wind and Light." *Fine Homebuilding* (March 1987): 87.

Rockhill, Dan. "A Concrete Belvedere." *Fine Homebuilding* (Jan. 1986): 64-9.

Rockhill, Dan. "Tom's Wonder Building." *Fine Homebuilding* (Jan. 1986): 72-5.

Rockhill, Dan. "A Compact Passive Solar House." *Fine Homebuilding* (May 1985): 72-7.

Rockhill, Dan. "The Deck Upstairs." *Fine Homebuilding* (Jan. 1983): 58-61.

Television

HGTV, "Offbeat America." Longhouse (Sept. 2005).

HGTV, "Offbeat America." Terrace House (Sept. 2005).

HGTV, "Dream Builders." Terrace House (July 2002).

HGTV, "Homes Across America." Kleinberg House (August 2000).

HGTV, "Homes Across America." Shimomura House (August 2000).

HGTV, "Dream Builders." Kleinberg House Process (March 1999).

HGTV, "Extreme Homes," Hillcrest House (June 1998).

Lectures +

Member, *Architecture* Magazine 'Home of the Year' Awards Jury (2005).

Lecture, North Carolina State University (Oct. 2005).

Judge, North Dakota Design Awards (Sept. 2005)

Kansas City AIA, Design/Build Presentation, Studio 804 (Sept. 2005).

Keynote Address, North Dakota Annual AIA, (Sept. 2005).

Design Build Institute, Midwest Region, Presentation (May 2005).

University of Wisconsin, Milwaukee (March 2005).

Paragraph Gallery Exhibition, Kansas City, Missouri (Jan. 2005).

Residential Architect Design Awards Jury, Washington, DC (Jan. 2005).

AIA Kansas/Kansas City Conference. Near the Edge: The Work of Rockhill and Associates (2004).

Member, Iowa Craftsmanship Awards Jury (2004).

Washington University of St. Louis (Sept. 2004).

University of Kentucky (March 2004).

Western Council of Architectural Registration Boards (March 2004).

Symposium: Thinking and Doing; The Role of Design/Build Studios in Architectural Education, Illinois Institute of Technology (Feb. 2004).

Oklahoma State University (Feb. 2004).

Clemson University (Nov. 2003).

Dalhousie University, Halifax, Nova Scotia (Oct. 2003).

University of Colorado (Oct. 2003).

Hallmark Design Group, Kansas City (Aug. 2003).

Rural Studio, Auburn University (March 2003).

Graham Foundation, Chicago (Dec. 2002).

Louisiana State University (Oct. 2002).

University of Arkansas (Oct. 2002).

Harvard University, "Practice Out There" (Summer 2002).

Keynote Address, Mid America Design Build Institute (April 2002).

Keynote Address, AIA/ACSA Experiences in Design Build (Feb. 2002).

Keynote Address, ACSA West Central Conference (Oct. 2000).

Keynote Address, Preservation Alliance, Constitution Hall (Sept. 2000).

Livable Cities, North Dakota AIA (Sept. 2000).

Crossing Boundaries, University of Notre Dame (April 2000).

University of Nebraska, School of Architecture (March 2000).

Masonry Conference, University of Kansas (March 2000).

AIAS Keynote Address, Annual Conference Central Region, Springfield, Missouri (March 2000).

University of Detroit, School of Architecture (Feb. 2000).

Young Architects Forum, Kansas City, Missouri (Jan. 2000).

AIA Kansas, Annual Conference, Design Forum, Topeka, Kansas (Oct. 1999).

Keynote Address, Award Banquet, North Dakota State University (April 1999).

Work Built, New and Old Club, Lawrence, Kansas (Dec. 1998).

Mississippi State University, Building Workshop (April 1998).

Preservation History, Washburn University (April 1997).

Architecture Club, El Dorado Inc., Kansas City (March 1996).

Masonry Conference, University of Kansas (March 1994).

Drury College, Springfield, Missouri (April 1993).

Southwest Louisiana State University (March 1993).

Web Sites

www.rockhillandassociates.com
www.studio804.com

The Firm

The Compagnons du Devoir, a traditional French Guild, sets
goals for its members of professional, moral and spiritual perfection
through manual work and the simultaneous nurturing of
consciousness. Jean Bernard, a present-day leader has written:

> From the beginning, man has been both manual and intellectual.
> Hand and mind have developed simultaneously without the
> former being the dregs of the other. The hand is not the vile
> instrument of the mind but its close associate, and generations
> pass down to one another, intermittent failures aside, the
> fruit of this union bestowed on man alone, the precious bequest
> [*le précieux dépôt*] slowly acquired that remains the just
> foundation of all education.[1]

Dan Rockhill, a graduate of Notre Dame University and the
M.Arch program at the State University of New York at Buffalo,
has been working at refining the art of design and construction
since his move to Kansas to teach at the University of Kansas in
1980. David Sain joined him in practice in 1989, and they have
worked together since that time on a wide variety of design and
construction projects. They seek to breathe life into work that
captures the pleasures of design and reflects a strong connection to
materiality; something that Rockhill calls "the presence of the hand."

1. Jean Bernard. *Le Compagnonnage: Rencontre de la jeunesse et de la tradition.*
   Paris: Presses Universitaires de France, 1972, p. 593 (translation by Gabriel Rockhill).

Chronological Index
of Projects

Contributors

Brian Carter

Brian Carter is an architect who worked in practice with Arup Associates in London prior to joining the University of Michigan, where he was Chair of Architecture from 1994 to 2001. He is currently Professor and Dean of the School of Architecture & Urban Planning at the State University of New York at Buffalo. His work has been published in numerous international journals, including *Casabella*, *Detail* and The *Architectural Review*. The author of several books, Brian Carter also initiated the MAP series, which won an AIA International Book Award.

Juhani Pallasmaa

Juhani Pallasmaa is an architect who has worked in practice since the early 1960s. He established Pallasmaa Architects in 1983 and in addition to designing buildings has been active in urban planning as well as product and graphic design. He has taught and lectured internationally and published numerous books and essays. In Finland Juhani Pallasma was Professor at the Helsinki University of Technology (1991-97), Director of the Museum of Finnish Architecture (1978-83) and Rector of the Institute of Industrial Arts, Helsinki. He has also held visiting professorships at the Washington University in St. Louis, University of Virginia and Yale University. His books include: *Encounters: Architectural Essays 1976-2000*, Helsinki 2004; *Sensuous Minimalism*, Beijing 2002; *The Architecture of Image: Existential Space in Cinema*, Helsinki 2001; *Alvar Aalto: Villa Mairea*, Helsinki, 1998; *The Eyes of the Skin*, London 1996; and *Animal Architecture*, Helsinki 1995.

Grant Wanzel

Grant Wanzel is Dean of the Faculty of Architecture & Planning at Dalhousie University and Chair of the Editorial Board of Tuns Press. He has practised community-based architecture in Halifax for many years and founded the Neighbourhood Housing Association – a non-profit housing developer. He has served on and chaired the boards of local and national housing organizations including the National Housing Committee of the Canadian Council on Social Development and the CMHC Graduate Studies Scholarship Committee. Professor Wanzel was a member of the Research and Policy Committee of the Canadian Housing and Renewal Association and served as President for two years. He has directed the work of the award-winning Creighton-Gerrish Development Association, a non-profit, community-based developer since 1995. He was awarded CMHC's National Social Housing Award in 1999 and received CMHC's 2001 Volunteer of the Year Award.

Tod Williams

Tod Williams received his undergraduate degree and Master of Fine Arts and Architecture from Princeton in 1965 and 1967 respectively. In 1982 he received an Advanced Fellowship from the American Academy in Rome and in 1992 he was made a Fellow in the American Institute of Architects.

The partnership of Tod Williams Billie Tsien and Associates was formed in 1986. Their work has been widely published and has received worldwide recognition.

Photo credits

Acknowledgements

p.8, left opening page of Brian Carter essay, Industrial Facades image: Bernd and Hiller Becher, Industrial Facades, 1970-1992. Fifteen black and white photographs, overall: 68 3/4" x 95" (installed as a group), Albright-Knox Gallery, Buffalo, NY. Sarah Norton Goodyear Fund, 1995.

p.9, top right of Brian Carter essay, Men of Progress image: Men of Progress. (l to r): William Thomas Green Morton, James Bogardus, Samuel Colt, Cyrus Hall McCormick, Joseph Saxton, Charles Goodyear, Peter Cooper, Jordan Lawrence Mott, Joseph Henry, Eliphalet Nott, John Ericsson, Frederick Sickels, Samuel Finley Breese Morse, Henry Burden, Richard March Hoe, Erastus Bigelow, Isaiah Jennings, Thomas Blanchard, Elias Howe. Christian Schussele, 1824-1879. Oil on canvas, 130.4 x 194.9 cm (51 3/8 x 76 3/4 in.), 1862. NPG.65.60 National Portrait Gallery, Smithsonian Institution; Transfer from the National Gallery of Art; Gift of Andrew W. Mellon, 1942.

Paul Bardagjy
68, 71, 73, 74, 75

Hobart Jackson
83, 85, 86, 87, 88, 89

p.98: Illustration from Frank Leslie's Illustrated Newspaper, July 26, 1856. Exterior view of Constitution Hall with Col. Edwin Vose Sumner dispersing the Free-State Legislature, Topeka, Kansas Territory, July 4, 1856.

All other photographs and drawings courtesy of Rockhill and Associates and Studio 804 Inc.

I would like to thank Dave Sain for his tremendous contribution, all of the current and former dedicated employees who have put up with long hours for low pay, and the students who have participated in the Studio 804 projects for no pay at all. The many clients who have engaged our services deserve special recognition for their appreciation of modern architecture. I would also like to thank Brian Carter for his encouragement, essay and editing, Grant Wanzel and Donald Westin at Tuns Press for their willingness to take on this project, Juhani Pallasmaa for his essay and Tod Williams for his postscript. Thank you to my KU colleague, Kent Speckelmeyer, for his support for the Studio 804 effort and most of all to my wife and family for putting up with the madness of never ending work.

DR

Also by Tuns Press:

Wood Design Awards 2004, ISBN 0-929112-52-0, 2005

Architecture Canada 2004: The Governor General's Medals in Architecture, ISBN 0-929112-51-2, 2004

Saucier + Perrotte Architectes, 1995-2002, ISBN 0-929112-46-6, 2004

Wood Design Awards 2003, ISBN 0-929112-50-4, 2003

Barry Johns Architects: Selected Projects 1984-1998, ISBN 0-929112-32-6, 2000

Brian MacKay-Lyons: Selected Projects 1986-1997, ISBN 0-929112-39-3, 1998

Works: The Architecture of A.J. Diamond, Donald Schmitt & Company, 1968-1995, ISBN 0-929112-31-8, 1996

Patkau Architects: Selected Projects 1983-1993, ISBN 0-929112-28-8, 1994

For additional information, please see our website at tunspress.dal.ca